COME THIS FAR
TO FREEDOM

A History of African Americans

COME THIS FAR TO
FREEDOM

A History of African Americans

by Angela Shelf Medearis

*Illustrated by **Terea D. Shaffer**
and with prints and photographs*

Atheneum   1993   New York

Maxwell Macmillan Canada
Toronto

Maxwell Macmillan International
New York   Oxford   Singapore   Sydney

Atheneum
Macmillan Publishing Company
866 Third Avenue
New York, NY 10022

Maxwell Macmillan Canada, Inc.
1200 Eglinton Avenue East
Suite 200
Don Mills, Ontario M3C 3N1

Macmillan Publishing Company is part of the Maxwell Communication Group of Companies.

First edition
Printed in the United States of America

10 9 8 7 6 5 4 3 2 1

The text of this book is set in Palatino.

Library of Congress Cataloging-in-Publication Data

Medearis, Angela Shelf, 1956–
    Come this far to freedom / by Angela Shelf Medearis ; illustrated by Terea D. Shaffer and with prints and photographs.—1st ed.
        p.   cm.
    Includes bibliographical references and index.
    Summary: Traces the history and accomplishments of African Americans as explorers, inventors, writers, soldiers, artists, scientists, and more, from the days of slavery to the present.
    ISBN 0-689-31522-8
    1. Afro-Americans—History—Juvenile literature. [1. Afro-Americans—History.
    2. Afro-Americans—Biography.] I. Shaffer, Terea D., ill. II. Title.
    E185.M38   1993
    973'.0496—dc20   92-31251

With love for Deanna, Kendra, Kenneth Ray, Michael, Courtney, Cameron, Marcy, Anysa, and children everywhere

America was founded on the basis of life, liberty, and the pursuit of happiness. No matter how your ancestors arrived here, no matter what color your skin is, no matter what language your great-grandparents spoke, we are all here and we are all Americans. With all America's faults, this land is still a wonderful place to live. Children, cherish this country, cherish your freedom, and hold on to your dreams.

A.S.M.

Midway

I've come this far to freedom and I won't turn back.
I'm climbing to the highway from my old dirt track.
    I'm coming and I'm going
    And I'm stretching and I'm growing
And I'll reap what I've been sowing or my skin's not black.

I've prayed and slaved and waited and I've sung my song.
You've bled me and you've starved me but I've still grown
strong.
    You've lashed me and you've treed me
    And you've everything but freed me
But in time you'll know you need me and it won't be long.

I've seen the daylight breaking high above the bough.
I've found my destination and I've made my vow;
    So whether you abhor me
    Or deride me or ignore me,
Mighty mountains loom before me and I won't stop now.

Naomi Long Madgett

From *Star by Star,* by Naomi Long Madgett. (Harlo Press, 1965; Evenill, 1970; reprinted by Lotus Press, Inc.) By permission of the author.

CONTENTS

IV A MOVEMENT FOR EQUALITY

V BREAKING DOWN THE BARRIERS

I

FROM HOMELAND TO HARDSHIP

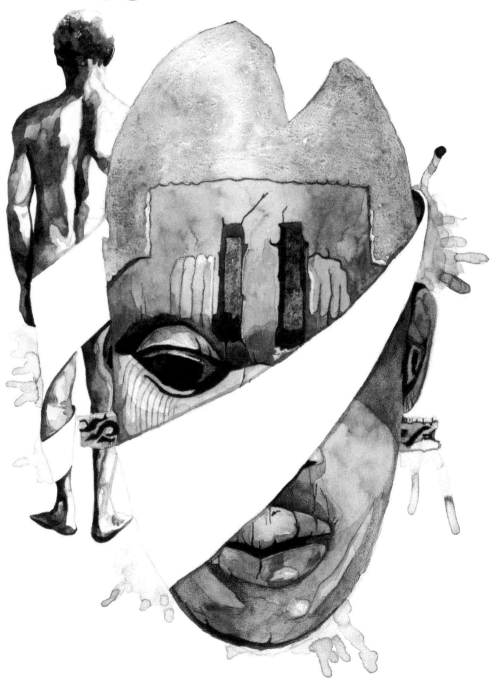

1

Africa

Africa is a vast land on the eastern side of the Atlantic Ocean. It is the second largest continent in the world, with an area of 11.5 million square miles.

Tiny tribal villages and big industrial cities, hot deserts and rainy, green jungles, icy, snowcapped mountains and long rivers are all part of the mixture of ancient and modern, old and new found in Africa. Traditional African music, literature, art, and dance have been preserved for hundreds of years.

From its rich earth Africa produces oil, metals, precious stones, rubber, tea, cocoa, and coffee. Many unusual animals also live in Africa.

Africa is a land of many languages, cultures, and tribes, the cradle of civilization, the starting place of history.

2

African Kings and Queens

For many years Africa was ruled by black kings and queens. There are still black kings, queens, and chiefs in power in many parts of Africa. Other African countries have a president and a government like the American government.

Hatshepsut, Nefertiti, Sheba, Nzingha, and Yaa Asantewa were ancient African queens.

Piankhi of Nubia, Taharqa of Egypt, Solomon, Ramses I and II, Shaka, Askia the Great of Songhai, and Haile Selassie were African kings. Black men and women have been rulers in Africa for hundreds of years.

3

Askia the Great (1444?–1538)

African King

Muhammad Abu Bakr was a general under King Sonni Ali in the kingdom of Songhai in West Africa. For many years he served King Ali faithfully in one battle after another. In 1469 they led their army against the rich city of Timbuktu and captured it. For seven years they plotted and fought against the warriors in Djenné, a city on the Niger River. King Ali and General Muhammad surrounded the river city with their navy. The people of Djenné finally surrendered because they could not get food or supplies.

Side by side, in battle after battle, King Ali and General Muhammad Abu Bakr led their army, which captured city after city. Soon Songhai was as large as Europe is today. When King Ali died in 1492, General Muhammad Abu Bakr took his place.

King Sonni Ali had many relatives who felt that the king's crown should rest upon their heads, but in 1493 Muhammad Abu Bakr won the right to the throne of Songhai. "Askia, askia!" ("Thief, thief!") cried Sonni Ali's relatives as Muhammad was crowned king. But Muhammad didn't let their name-calling or anything else stop him from ruling. As a matter of fact, one of the first things King Muhammad did was change his name to

Askia! The king who was called a thief became known throughout history as Askia the Great.

In 1495 King Askia traveled to the powerful kingdom of Egypt. He wanted to learn more about how to rule and govern his own kingdom. For two years King Askia studied with the African doctors, mathematicians, scientists, and scholars who lived there.

When King Askia returned to Songhai, he used his education to make his kingdom a better place. King Askia strongly believed in education for his people. Students from all over Africa came to the University of Sankore in Timbuktu to study law and surgery.

King Askia divided Songhai into equal parts. Then he chose wise men called *fari* to govern each part. Men called *noi*, or chiefs, ruled the large cities. This allowed King Askia to spend most of his time warring on other kingdoms. He made his prisoners into a slave army and led them in battle. His soldiers wore chain mail armor. Their weapons were swords and iron lances. King Askia and his army conquered most of the great African empires of his day. His kingdom grew wealthier and larger with every victory.

King Askia improved the banking and credit system of Songhai. He also set a standard for weights, measures, and scales. This way, none would be cheated when they came to buy and sell their goods at the marketplace. European and Asian merchants came to Songhai in great numbers. The merchants of Songhai traded their slaves and other goods for guns, gunpowder, rum, and cloth. Songhai became a rich kingdom filled with books, music, dancing, and poetry.

Askia the Great was nearly ninety years old when his reign ended. As he grew older, he lost his eyesight. Then the Moors began to war against the people of Songhai, and the mighty kingdom was defeated. Terrible tribal wars and the slave trade changed the great empire of Songhai and Africa forever.

4

The Slave Trade

Slavery began hundreds of years before America was discovered. Under the laws of ancient Africa one person could own another person. Selling and trading prisoners of war was an African custom. Anyone who was in debt could be sold into slavery to pay his bills.

More than 40 million black people were taken from Africa during the years of the slave trade.

Slavery became a big business when African kings found they could sell or trade their slaves to European slave traders in exchange for rum, guns, cloth, and other goods. Now, not only prisoners of war and debtors were enslaved. Sometimes African slave traders would raid villages and kidnap the people who lived there. The captives were held in prisons called barracoons until the slave ships arrived. Then the captives were examined, sold, and packed into a small space in the bottom of the ship. After many days the ship landed in the West Indies or North America. The African captives were sold as slaves to the Europeans living there.

In 1619 twenty Africans arrived in Jamestown, Virginia, aboard a Dutch ship. The Africans were originally going to the West Indies to be sold as slaves. It is not known why the captain of the ship set sail for America. When he arrived in Jamestown, the captain pretended he was in need of food. He traded the Africans to the settlers for food and supplies. These captives were probably indentured as servants for seven years and then given their freedom. Many white indentured servants paid their passage to America this way.

As America grew and more workers were needed, Virginia, Massachusetts, Connecticut, Maryland, New York, and other colonies voted to make slavery legal. More than forty million black people were taken from Africa during the years of the slave trade. Twenty million came to America. Millions died during slave raids, on board slave ships, and on plantations. Buying and selling Africans became a business. Using Africans as slaves became a way of life in America.

Olaudah Equiano was a Nigerian prince. When he was about ten years old he and his sister were captured and sold into slavery. Olaudah and his sister were among the millions of Africans who were taken from their homes and families and sold into slavery in America.

5

Olaudah Equiano (1745?–1797)

(Gustavus Vassa) Abolitionist

One morning when Ibo chief Equiano and his wife were away, two men and a woman from another tribe silently slipped over a wall and into their home. Slave traders! Before their son, Olaudah, and their daughter could escape, the men covered their mouths and took them away into the jungle. The children were sold and separated.

After a long and weary journey overland, the slave traders and the young boy reached a ship that was anchored at sea.

Olaudah Equiano was the son of an African chief. He was captured at the age of ten by slave traders and sold into slavery. His name was changed to Gustavus Vassa. Equiano wrote a book about his experiences in 1789.

Many other Africans were on board the ship. Some were crying, others were moaning. All the captives were chained together. When Olaudah saw the big ship and the strange-looking men he was terrified. He thought he was going to be eaten alive! He was so frightened that he fainted.

The slave traders took Olaudah down to the bottom of the ship. So many Africans were packed together in the small space that it was hard to breathe. The crying and moaning were deafening, and the smell was horrible. Olaudah became sick and refused to eat. Because he would not eat he was beaten. It was one of the most terrible times of his life. Other captives from the Ibo tribe told Olaudah that the slave traders were going to take them all away from their people and their homes and put them to work.

When the ship arrived in America, Olaudah was sold to an Englishman living there named Michael Henry Pascal. He changed Olaudah's name to Gustavus Vassa. Olaudah was known as Gustavus Vassa, a slave, from that day on. But, deep inside, Olaudah knew that he was an Ibo prince, the son of an African chief.

Pascal promised that one day he would set Gustavus free. In 1762, after serving Pascal for many years, Gustavus asked for his freedom. Pascal became very angry. He was so angry that he sold Gustavus to the first person who offered to buy him, James Doran, captain of the ship *Charming Sally.* Later Doran sold Gustavus to Robert King, a Quaker. King promised Gustavus that he would allow him to buy his freedom. Gustavus worked very hard for King and also took on many odd jobs to earn money. In 1766, after buying his freedom from King, Gustavus left America and moved to England. While living in England, Equiano wrote a letter to the queen begging her to abolish slavery in the West Indies, which was under English rule. In 1789 Equiano wrote a two-volume book about his life entitled *Interesting Narrative of the Life of Olaudah Equiano or Gustavus Vassa the African.* This book was one of the first ever written by a former slave about the slave trade. Gustavus wanted everyone to know the truth about his terrible voyage to America and the horrors of slavery.

6
The Middle Passage

The voyage from Africa to America has been called the middle passage. Africa was the beginning. The trip across the waters was the middle. The West Indies or America was the end of the journey for the African captives.

During the journey from Africa to America, hundreds of Africans were crowded into the ship's small storage space. Many of the captives died from diseases during these terrible journeys.

The slave traders tried to take as many Africans as possible on board their ships. Sometimes four hundred captives were crowded into the ship's small storage space. Because of the cramped space the captives were unable to sit up or stand. For days at a time they were forced to stay in one position. They were given very little water or food. There was very little air to breathe. The hard wooden floor and the chains on their wrists and ankles rubbed their skin and flesh down to the bone. There was only a small bucket for a bathroom. The small, airless space soon became filthy. Many of the captives died from diseases during these terrible journeys.

7

Mutiny at Sea

Some African captives refused to become slaves. Hundreds of captives jumped into the sea or starved themselves to death. Others fought the slave traders and took over the ship. Joseph Cinque was captured and sold into slavery in 1839. He was taken aboard the slave ship *Amistad* along with fifty-two others.

After a few days Cinque found a nail and was able to pick the lock on his neck irons. He freed himself and the other captives from their chains. Then he led them in the takeover of the ship.

Only two slave traders were spared, Jose Ruiz and Pedro Montes. Cinque demanded to be taken back to Africa. Ruiz and Montes sailed toward Africa by day but changed their course at night. After two months on a zigzag course, the *Amistad* finally landed in Long Island, New York. Cinque and the other Africans were arrested and brought to trial.

Former president John Quincy Adams represented Cinque

and the other captives before the U.S. Supreme Court. Cinque was called to the witness stand. He spoke very little English; but with great emotion he acted out his capture and sale, and the incident on the *Amistad,* for the jury. The jurors found the captives not guilty!

On November 27, 1841, Cinque and the surviving captives set sail for their African homeland. This was very unusual. Millions of enslaved Africans never saw their homeland or their families again. Most of the African captives were sold into slavery on the auction block.

8

The Auction Block

After the African captives reached America they were sold the same way a horse, or wagon, or a piece of farmland is bought and sold—on the auction block.

The slave buyers would gather at a special place in the city. Then they examined the captives the way they looked at a horse or a cow. Fathers, mothers, children, and families were sold separately, in pairs, or together.

Morris Hillyer, a former slave, recalled during an interview about his life as a slave that "every first Tuesday, slaves were brought in from Virginia and sold on the block. The auctioneer was Cap'n Dorsey. E. M. Cobb was the slave-bringer. They would stand the slave up on the block and talk about what a fine-looking specimen of black manhood or womanhood they was, tell how healthy they was, look in their mouth and examine their teeth just like they was a horse, and talk about the kind of work they would be fit for and could do."

As slaves, the Africans had no rights or freedom. They were

GANG OF 25 SEA ISLAND
COTTON AND RICE NEGROES,
By LOUIS DE SAUSSURE.

On THURSDAY the 25th Sept., 1852, at 11 o'clock, A.M., will be sold at RYAN'S MART, in Chalmers Street, in the City of Charleston,

A prime gang of 25 Negroes, accustomed to the culture of Sea Island Cotton and Rice.

CONDITIONS.—One-half Cash, balance by Bond, bearing interest from day of sale, payable in one and two years, to be secured by a mortgage of the negroes and approved personal security.   Purchasers to pay for papers.

Advertisement for captured Africans to be sold on an auction block in Charleston, South Carolina

forced to learn a strange new language. They were given new names. They were made to work long hours without pay. Life was hard for the African captives in this new land.

9
The Cotton Kingdom

One reason that slavery grew in America is that a large work-force was needed in the South. In 1793 Eli Whitney invented a cotton gin. The cotton gin could remove the tiny seeds, hulls, and other debris that were found in cotton bolls. The gin "combed" out the seeds and other objects in the cotton,

Between 1619 and 1863, millions of slaves were purchased to work as laborers.

leaving the cotton fiber clean. Cotton became one of the major crops in the South. The more cotton planted and sold, the more money the farmer could make. Between 1619 and 1863, millions of slaves were purchased to work in the fields and pick cotton.

England also demanded more and more cotton for use in its textile mills. The water-powered loom was a new invention that replaced most of the hand weaving that had been done in the past. The spinning jenny was a device that made it possible to twist cotton fibers into thread much faster than the old way, which was by hand.

Before the invention of the cotton gin, water-powered loom, and spinning jenny, cotton farmers in Richmond, Virginia, were able to sell only thirty large bags of cotton a year to England. After these inventions were created, the farmers in one year sold over thirty *million* pounds of cotton to England.

FIGHTING FOR FREEDOM

10

America's Fight for Freedom

In 1770 America was still ruled by England. The American Revolution was fought to free America from English rule. Most American colonists did not want to be ruled by, or pay any tax money to, England.

Crispus Attucks was the first to die at the Boston Massacre in the struggle for America's freedom in 1770.

In 1750 Crispus Attucks ran away from his master. He became a sailor in Boston, Massachusetts. On March 5, 1770, Attucks was with a group of men who were angry about the British troops that King George III of England had sent to Boston. Attucks and the other men threw ice, snowballs, sticks, and stones at the soldiers. The British soldiers opened fire upon the crowd. Attucks was the first to die, along with four other men. This incident has been called the Boston Massacre.

At this time a master could send a slave to fight for him if he was called to war. The slave was usually given his freedom when he replaced his master on the battlefield. Thousands of black men fought in the revolutionary war and many gave their lives for America's freedom. Prince Hall, Salem Poor, Oliver Cromwell, and Peter Salem all fought during the American Revolution.

11

Peter Salem (1750–1816)

Soldier, Revolutionary War

America and England were at war and soldiers were needed to fight for America. Free blacks were allowed to serve. Slaves were only allowed to join the army as replacements for their masters. Peter Salem's master promised to free Peter in exchange for his service during the American Revolution. Salem was proud to be a part of a group of American soldiers called the Minutemen. These men were trained to be ready to fight at a minute's notice. Salem fought along with the other Minutemen during the battle at Concord against the British soldiers. After the battle at Concord, Salem received his freedom. Later he enlisted in the Fifth Massachusetts Regiment under Colonel John Nixon.

On June 17, 1775, English major John Pitcairn led a group of British soldiers into battle against the American troops. Salem

Peter Salem was among the thousands of black men who fought during the American Revolution.

and the other soldiers fired upon the British soldiers. The British soldiers retreated, returned to fight, and retreated again. When Major Pitcairn stood to lead his men into battle again, it is fairly certain that Peter Salem's shot killed him. This fight was called the Battle of Bunker Hill. It was one of the bloodiest battles of the American Revolution.

On July 4, 1776, America declared its independence from England. This new freedom was greatly celebrated in America, but it was a sad time for black people. Thomas Jefferson had written a paragraph for the Declaration of Independence pointing out the evils of slavery, but in the end it was taken out. Although many black men like Peter Salem fought for America's freedom, most black people were still slaves.

12

Uprisings and Rebellions

All over America black men and women declared that they'd "rather die free than live as a slave." Battles between slaves and their masters happened more and more often. The news of a slave revolt in a far-off place called Haiti was whispered from one slave to another.

After many years of slavery the Haitians declared war on their French masters in August 1791. They elected a fellow slave, François-Dominique Toussaint-L'Ouverture, as their general. Toussaint led his Haitian troops in battle after battle against the English, Spanish, and French armies. The Haitians won their freedom in 1793. On November 28, 1803, the war was over, but the battle to remain free continued. L'Ouverture was captured and died while in a French prison. The leaders of slave rebellions in America patterned themselves after L'Ouverture. Gabriel Pros-

Toussaint-L'Ouverture was the leader of the Haitian slave revolt for freedom from the French.

ser, Nat Turner, and Denmark Vesey were black men who led American slave rebellions. Denmark Vesey particularly admired Toussaint-L'Ouverture. He planned a slave rebellion in South Carolina in 1822 that he hoped would make American blacks as free as the people of Haiti.

13

Denmark Vesey (1767–1822)

Slave Rebellion Leader

For more than twenty years Denmark Vesey was the slave of a slave trader, traveling with his master to Africa and the West Indies to buy and sell slaves. But Vesey himself hated the very thought of slavery. One lucky day in 1799 Vesey won $1,500 in a lottery and used some of the money to buy his freedom.

After becoming a free man Vesey worked as a carpenter in Charleston, South Carolina. He was able to make a good living in Charleston and to buy some land. He became wealthy and respected. He was also a minister in the new all-black African Methodist church. The African Methodist church was founded in Philadelphia in 1787 by Richard Allen, a free black minister. From time to time Vesey heard news of slave uprisings in other states and in other countries. He decided that the only way to end slavery was for black people to band together and fight. For months he quietly talked with slave field hands about fighting for their freedom. Then he carefully planned the battle and set the date of the uprising for July 16, 1822.

Vesey recruited an army of more than nine thousand field slaves. As soon as they got the signal from Vesey they were to be ready to attack. Vesey didn't trust slaves who worked in the homes of whites, and he didn't want any house servants in his army. He instructed his followers not to reveal any of their plans

to house servants. But one of Vesey's followers disobeyed his instructions and told a house servant about the uprising. Before Vesey could begin the battle, the house servant revealed what he knew to the city officials of Charleston! Vesey had prepared for a problem like this by telling no one but his closest followers the whole battle plan. He continued to act as though nothing had happened. Then someone else close enough to him to have names of those involved and the dates of the battles reported Vesey to the city officials. He was arrested, along with his assistants, Ned and Rolla Bennett, Peter Poyas, and "Gullah Jack" Pritchard.

Denmark Vesey and more than thirty others were hanged at Blake's Landing in Charleston on July 2, 1822. Vesey's plans for liberty may have failed, but the struggle for freedom for black people continued.

14
Abolitionists Fight Against Slavery

Many people wanted to end slavery in America. They felt that the Declaration of Independence made all men equal, and they wanted everyone to be free. They were called abolitionists because they wanted to abolish, or end, slavery.

Both black and white abolitionists worked to end slavery in America, fighting against slavery in many ways. Many abolitionists hid runaway slaves in their homes. Helping a runaway slave was a crime. Abolitionists were often beaten or put in prison, and their homes and businesses burned. Some abolitionists were killed because they spoke out against slavery.

Sojourner Truth was a powerful speaker against the injustice of slavery.

25

Abolitionist Harriet Beecher Stowe wrote *Uncle Tom's Cabin*, a book about the evils of slavery. *Uncle Tom's Cabin* was one of the best-selling books of all time. Frances E. W. Harper, Henry Wadsworth Longfellow, and Walt Whitman wrote poems against slavery. Abolitionists also printed newspapers and pamphlets and gave speeches.

Abolitionists were of different races and religions but held in common the belief in freedom for all people. Thomas Garrett and Levi Coffin were of the Quaker religion. David Ruggles, Sojourner Truth, and Frederick Douglass were famous black abolitionists.

15

Frederick Douglass (1817–1895)

Reformer, Journalist

When Frederick Douglass was a baby, his mother was sold to the owner of a plantation twelve miles away. Young Frederick was left behind in his grandmother's care. He was only able to see his mother a few times after she was sold. He never saw his father at all.

When Frederick was ten years old he was taught to read a little by his master's daughter. When her husband found out about the classes he made her stop. It was a crime to teach a slave to read or to write.

Frederick practiced the letters and words he'd learned by copying them on a wall with a piece of chalk whenever he had the chance. He knew that being able to read and write was a priceless gift.

When Frederick was a teenager he was sent to work for a cruel man named Edward Covey. He was beaten every night. One day Frederick decided that he wasn't going to take any

Frederick Douglass was an editor, abolitionist, and statesman. He gave speeches and wrote articles about slavery. Douglass used his print shop as a station on the Underground Railroad.

more beatings. The next time Covey tried to hit him, Frederick threw the man on the ground and beat him! Covey never struck Frederick again, but he still tried to work him to death.

When Frederick was twenty-one years old he was sent to work on the shipping docks. He fell in love with Anna Murray, a young, free black woman. He wanted to marry his sweetheart and live in freedom, too, so he decided to run away. A free black sailor helped Frederick escape. Anna and Frederick were married and lived in New Bedford, in the free state of Massachusetts.

Frederick joined an abolitionists' group in Massachusetts. He had a wonderful speaking voice and lectured against slavery everywhere he went. At first he was afraid his master would find him and take him back into slavery. But he decided to take the chance.

It was very dangerous for anyone to speak against slavery. Sometimes people threatened to kill Frederick. Men often threw things at him during his speeches. After one speech Douglass was thrown down a flight of steps. He suffered many beatings and broken bones, but that didn't stop him from speaking out.

In August 1845 Frederick Douglass traveled to the British Isles, where he gave speeches about the evils of slavery. English abolitionists gave Frederick enough money to start a newspaper. When Frederick returned to Massachusetts he opened a print shop and began publishing his newspaper. At first Frederick named his paper the *North Star;* then he changed the name to *Frederick Douglass's Paper.* He wrote many articles about slavery and used his printshop as a station on the Underground Railroad. More than four hundred slaves escaped to freedom in Canada with his help.

16

The Underground Railroad

In 1831 Tice Davids, a slave, decided to run away. His master tried to catch Tice and bring him back to Kentucky. But when Tice crossed the Ohio River, he disappeared from sight! His master spent many hours looking for him but never found him. When he returned to Kentucky he told people that Tice must have disappeared on "an underground road."

Tice Davids did not really find an underground road. He was hidden by a group of abolitionists in Ohio. Many slaves ran away from their masters and the plantations in the South to the free states in the North. Some slaves traveled all the way to Canada to be free.

Indian tribes often helped hide runaway slaves, and many abolitionist groups helped slaves reach freedom. After 1831 the

abolitionists began to use railroad terms when talking about runaways. Abolitionists were "agents" on the Underground Railroad. A runaway slave was called a "package." When a slave ran away he was "taking a ticket on the Underground Railroad." A man or woman who led a runaway slave to the North was called a "conductor." A conductor went into the South to lead slaves north to freedom. This was very dangerous. A conductor had to be very brave and very clever to lead runaway slaves safely out of the South. Robert T. Hickman, John Fairfield, and Harriet Tubman were conductors on the Underground Railroad.

17

Harriet Tubman (1821–1913)

Abolitionist, Nurse, Scout, Spy

When Harriet Tubman was a teenager she was hit in the head with a piece of metal because she refused to chase a runaway slave. Harriet became very sick and often suffered from dizziness and sudden sleeping spells. The master of the plantation wanted to sell her, but no one wanted to buy a sick slave.

After many months Harriet regained her health, but she continued to suffer from dizziness and sleeping spells for the rest of her life.

After Harriet's master died it was decided that the plantation and all the slaves would be sold. Harriet's two sisters

Harriet Tubman led more than three hundred slaves to freedom on the Underground Railroad.

were sold first. When Harriet heard whispers that she was to be sold along with two of her brothers, she and her brothers decided to run away to the North.

The little group had only traveled for a few miles when the two young men became afraid. Runaway slaves were treated cruelly if they were caught. Harriet's brothers decided to go back to the plantation before they were missed. But Harriet would not turn back. She continued alone on the long, hard journey to freedom, using the North Star as her guide. She also received help along the way from members of the Underground Railroad.

After many days she reached the free state of Pennsylvania. "I looked at my hand," said Harriet, "to see if I was the same person now that I was free. There was such a glory over everything, the sun came like gold through the trees, and over the fields. I felt like I was in heaven!"

Harriet decided to lead other slaves to this glorious freedom. She became a conductor on the Underground Railroad. Harriet made many dangerous trips to lead her people from slavery in the South to freedom in the North. She helped over three hundred slaves escape from slavery, including her mother, father, brothers, and sisters. She made the slave owners so angry that they promised to pay forty thousand dollars to anyone who could capture her and bring her to the South, dead or alive.

Sometimes while Harriet was leading runaway slaves to freedom, some members of the group would become afraid, but she never allowed anyone to go back. She would pull out her pistol and aim it at the fearful one. "You'll be free or die," she said.

Harriet often used disguises and other tricks to fool slave catchers and she was never captured. She was proud of her record as a conductor on the Underground Railroad. "I never lost a passenger," she said, "and my train never ran off the track."

18

The Fugitive Slave Law

On September 18, 1850, Congress passed the Fugitive Slave Law. This law allowed a former slave owner to recapture a runaway slave even in a free state. Thomas Sims and Anthony Burns were runaway slaves who were living as free men in Boston. Their southern masters had them arrested and taken back to the South as slaves. Because of the Fugitive Slave Law, a runaway could not truly be free in America.

Canada did not allow slavery and wouldn't return escaped slaves to their masters. Hundreds of runaways made the long, hard journey to freedom in Canada. The cold Canadian winters and the lack of food and clothing made life very hard for them.

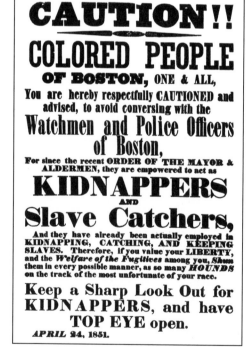

On September 18, 1850, Congress passed the Fugitive Slave Law. This law allowed a slave owner to recapture a runaway slave even in a free state. This poster was used to warn runaway slaves about slave catchers.

19

The Civil War

Slavery divided America into two parts. Most of the Northern states had ended slavery by 1804. Most of the states in the South were slave states.

America was growing. New states were forming. Abolitionists did not want slavery in the new states. Those who wanted slavery to continue demanded the new states be slave states. In 1861 the argument between the Northern and Southern states turned into war, the Civil War.

On January 1, 1863, President Abraham Lincoln issued the Emancipation Proclamation, which ended slavery in the Southern states involved in the Civil War. He also allowed black men

One hundred eighty-six thousand black men fought during the Civil War, and many died. Nearly three thousand were killed in battle, twenty-six thousand died from diseases.

to enlist in the military. In 1865 the North won the war. That same year the Thirteenth Amendment to the Constitution, which ended slavery in America, was passed and ratified. Jubilee! All black people were free!

Black men and women played an important part in fighting the Civil War. Harriet Tubman became a scout, spy, nurse, and cook for the Union army. Sergeant William Carney and the soldiers of the Fifty-fourth Massachusetts Infantry were among the 185,000 blacks who fought for their freedom as Union soldiers.

20

William H. Carney (1840–1908)

Sergeant, Company C, Fifty-fourth Infantry

When William Carney was a teenager his master died, and his family was freed. The Carney family moved from Virginia to New Bedford, Massachusetts.

Now that he was free, Carney couldn't decide what he wanted to do with his life. He worked at several odd jobs around New Bedford. He often thought about becoming a minister. Then the Civil War started and Carney decided to volunteer.

When the Civil War began, thousands of black men volunteered for military duty. Frederick Douglass asked President Lincoln to free all the slaves immediately. At first President Lincoln refused to end slavery or to let blacks enlist in the military. Lincoln was afraid that if he freed the slaves Kentucky, Missouri, Maryland, and Delaware, the southern border states, would leave the Union and fight for the Confederacy. It wasn't until 1863 that black soldiers and sailors were allowed to fight against slavery and the Confederacy.

These men served as cooks, laborers, and mule team drivers during the early months of the Civil War. Black men were not allowed to fight for their freedom until 1862.

On February 17, 1863, Carney joined Company C of the Fifty-fourth Massachusetts Infantry, the very first black troops to be organized for the Union army. Soon after the company was organized, its commander, Robert G. Shaw, received orders to march to South Carolina to attack Fort Wagner.

It was a terrible battle. Many soldiers were killed or wounded. Then the company's flag carrier was shot! Before the flag touched the ground Carney grabbed it. He ran with the flag to the front of the column. Even though he received a shot in the thigh and fell to his knees, he held the flag high. Carney was hurt so badly that at first he couldn't move. He stayed on

*Led by Colonel Robert Gould Shaw, the Fifty-fourth
Massachusetts Infantry fought at the assault on Fort
Wagner in 1863.*

his knees for over an hour while bullets whistled all around
him. The Fifty-fourth Infantry was forced to retreat. Carney
crept on one knee back to the line of safety. Before he could
reach his company, he was shot twice more.

The soldiers cheered when they saw Carney still holding
up the flag. "Boys," said Carney, "the old flag never touched
the ground!" Carney was awarded the Congressional Medal
of Honor for bravery. After the war, Carney, like many other
African Americans, began a new career. He became a mail carrier and messenger at the State House in Boston.

A new day was beginning for both blacks and whites, North-
erners and Southerners in America.

III
A FRESH START

21
Reconstruction

The end of the Civil War brought many changes to the South. It was a time of rebuilding, or reconstruction. The Reconstruction period was a difficult time for whites and blacks. The Civil War left many people in poverty. The Towns, farms, houses, and fields had been damaged. too

The Freedmen's Bureau gave clothing, food, medicine, and other help to the newly freed slaves.

Thousands of blacks left the South and moved North. Some free blacks started small farms, others moved into town. Many black families had been separated by slavery. Husbands, wives, mothers, fathers, and children began searching for one another.

The government started the Freedmen's Bureau to help newly freed black people get an education, register to vote, and find homes and jobs. The Freedmen's Bureau also gave out clothing, food, and medicine.

For the first time, black people in the South were free to vote, go to school, and go to church. Black people used their right to vote to elect Pinckney Pinchback, Hiram R. Revels, Robert Smalls, and other black politicians to office. Black men served as government officials for the first time.

22

Robert Smalls (1839–1915)

Civil War Hero, Congressman

When the Civil War began, Robert Smalls was forced to work for the Confederate navy. He became a pilot on a boat called the *Planter*.

Most of the crew on the *Planter* were slaves. Smalls knew that they could all be free if they could safely sail to the north side of the Charleston Bay. The Northern navy was there, only seven miles away, blockading the harbor.

Smalls and the other crew members were determined to take a chance on freedom. They waited until the captain left the *Planter* for the night. Then Smalls nervously put on the captain's broad-brimmed hat. He would have to fool the Southern soldiers stationed in the harbor watchtowers into thinking that he was the *Planter*'s captain. If he did not, the Southern soldiers would fire at the ship and try to stop it.

Robert Smalls was a Civil War hero, and a congressman in 1874.

Robert Smalls on the deck of the captured boat, the Planter

Smalls and the other men smuggled their wives and families aboard. Then Smalls, his wife, their two children, and thirteen others set sail for freedom. First they had to sail past the Confederate cannons. As they passed the Confederate fort Smalls loudly called out orders just like the captain. The Confederate sentry let them pass!

When they reached the Union side of the Charleston Bay, Smalls lowered the Confederate flag. Then he raised the white flag of truce. The Northern soldiers held their fire as the *Planter* came near. Smalls surrendered the *Planter* to the commander of the Union army. He, his family, and their friends were finally free! President Lincoln gave Smalls a reward for bringing the boat to the Union side. He was named its captain and was given his own crew. Smalls spent the rest of the Civil War fighting against the Southern navy.

After the North won the war Smalls became a politician. He was elected to Congress in 1874. Some members of Congress did not want any black men in office. They made it very hard for Smalls to represent the people who had elected him.

The Civil War brought slavery to an end, but life was still hard for black people in America.

23

Another Kind of Slavery

After the war a new way of operating farms and plantations was started in the South. The new way was called sharecropping. Most blacks still could not afford to buy their own land. Most of their former masters could not afford to pay the freed blacks for their labor. Under a sharecropping deal, the land was usually owned by whites and farmed by free blacks. Part of the

Many newly freed blacks became sharecroppers. It was a very hard way to make a living.

money from selling the crop would pay the "rent" for use of the land.

Sometimes the black farmers would have to get credit at the white-owned store to buy food and supplies until the crop came in. The prices at the store could be very high. Often the crop didn't produce as much as expected, or the weather was bad and ruined the crop. That meant that the money from the crop wouldn't be enough to pay the landowner or the store.

Black sharecroppers worked year after year but seldom made enough money to pay off their debt to the landowner and the store or to buy their own land. They could not leave their share because they owed money to the landowner and the store. Every year black sharecroppers in the South became poorer and poorer. For many black people, sharecropping became another kind of slavery.

24

New Laws and New Fears

New laws called "Black Codes" were created in the South after the Civil War. These laws took away most of the freedom black people had been given. Black people called these new laws "Jim Crow laws." "Jump Jim Crow" was a song and dance during slavery days. The verse of the song "Jump Jim Crow" went:

I jump around and spin around and do just so
But everytime I turn around I jump Jim Crow.

It seemed that every time a black person in the South turned around there was a strict new law. These new laws made life very hard. A black person had to have a pass to travel. Some-

"Daddy" Rice made the song and dance "Jim Crow" very popular after the Civil War. Black people began calling the harsh new laws "Jim Crow" laws.

The Knights of the White Camellia and the Ku Klux Klan sprang up after the Civil War. These groups terrorized the black community.

times black orphan children were turned over to whites to work until they became adults. In some Southern states a black person could not go out on the streets after sundown. A black person who tried to vote was often threatened or killed.

White mobs, like the Knights of the White Camellia and the Ku Klux Klan, began to burn and to kill to keep black people from obtaining equal rights with white citizens. Hate and fear spread across the land. Ida B. Wells-Barnett was a young woman who found a way to fight against this injustice. Ida didn't use her fists or a gun. Ida fought against racism with her pen.

25

Ida B. Wells-Barnett (1862–1931)

Journalist, Civil Rights Leader

Ida B. Wells, a young schoolteacher, had bought a ticket to Memphis, Tennessee. Ida was returning to school after a visit with her family. She found a seat on the train and sat down.

Whites and blacks paid the same price for a train ticket, but they did not receive the same treatment on the train. The "whites only" section of the train was clean and roomy. The "colored only" section was dirty, smoky, and crowded. Blacks and whites were not allowed to sit in the same train car or wait in the same waiting room at the train station.

Ida B. Wells-Barnett was a civil rights worker and journalist, and one of the founding members of the National Association for the Advancement of Colored People.

When the conductor came around to collect the tickets he told Ida that she was in the "whites only" section. Ida told the conductor that she wasn't going to move because she'd paid to sit there. The conductor demanded that Ida move to the "colored" section of the train. Although she was very small, Ida was not at all afraid of the conductor. When the conductor grabbed Ida by the arm, she bit him. The angry conductor found two other men to help him. They picked Ida up and put her off at the very next station!

Ida decided to fight back. She hired a lawyer and took her case to court. Ida also wrote a story about the incident for the *Living Way,* a church newspaper. Soon black newspapers all over the country were printing copies of Ida's story. Ida began writing other articles under the pen name Iola. Some people called her Iola, Princess of the Press. Ida became so successful that she was hired as a regular reporter by the Reverend William J. Simmons, editor of the Negro Press Association.

Ida wrote articles about the hard life black people led. She often wrote about the old, outdated books and materials black children had to use at school, and the harsh treatment black people received from the law. Ida still taught school during the day, but at night she was a newspaper editor. She had saved enough money from teaching school to become part owner of the *Memphis Free Speech and Headlight.*

The Memphis school board did not like Ida's newspaper article about the conditions in her school. In 1891 the board fired her. Ida was upset that she was punished for speaking the truth. Losing her teaching job didn't stop her from writing, though. Her articles helped to sell hundreds of copies of the *Memphis Free Speech and Headlight.* More and more black people began to buy her paper. They wanted to find out about the terrible crimes that were being committed against black people in the South. Ida made it a policy always to tell the truth, no matter what.

One night a terrible thing happened that changed Ida's whole life. Three black men, Thomas Moss, Calvin McDowell, and Henry Stewart, were murdered (or lynched, as it's sometimes called) by a mob of people. These three men owned Peoples Grocery Store. Their store was very successful and had more customers than a white-owned store in the same neighborhood. This made the white grocery store owner angry. One night a mob took Moss, McDowell, and Stewart outside the city limits and shot them to death.

Ida wrote a story about the murder of these men. She told her readers that if black people couldn't get justice in Tennessee then they should move west. Thousands of black people did just that. Blacks in Memphis saved their money so they could move. They stopped using streetcars and also stopped buying furniture and clothing. Then, when they had enough money, they quit their jobs and moved west. Every year more black people left the South.

Ida's articles made some whites so angry that they tore up her newspaper office and wrecked the building. They said that if she ever tried to publish her newspaper again she would be killed. Luckily, Ida was out of town when this happened. She wanted to go back to Memphis to protest this treatment, but her friends warned her not to come home.

Ida finally settled in Chicago, Illinois. While she was in Chicago she helped to organize several clubs for black women to serve the black community. These women's clubs were named after Ida and many are still in operation today. Ida also started the Alpha Suffrage Club in Chicago, which fought for the right of women to vote.

For years Ida secretly collected facts about the lynchings in the South. In 1895 she published a book called *A Red Record*. *A Red Record* was a list of every lynching Ida had information about. As chairman of the Anti-Lynching League, Ida also voiced her complaints to President William McKinley. She began to travel around the United States and to England to let people know the truth about the lynchings in America.

On June 27, 1895, Ida married Ferdinand Lee Barnett, a

lawyer and newspaper editor. She became the mother of four children. She continued to work tirelessly to find a solution to the racial problems in America. For many black people, it seemed best to do what Ida suggested: leave the South and move west.

26

Going West

In 1879 thousands of black people moved away from the states with the Jim Crow laws, the Black Codes, the Ku Klux Klan, and the lynchings. The western states seemed to be a place where black people could make a fresh start.

Lieutenant Henry O. Flipper was a member of a crack unit of black soldiers in the Tenth Cavalry stationed in the West. These soldiers were highly regarded by the native Americans

Mary Fields ran a stagecoach and mail route in the old West.

because of their skill and courage. They protected the settlers who were moving into native American territory in the West. Because of the soldiers' clothing and curly black hair, the natives named the soldiers after the buffalo, an animal they respected. The soldiers wore buffalo skin coats in the winter and had a picture of the buffalo on their uniforms. The soldiers of the Ninth and Tenth cavalries and the Twenty-fourth and Twenty-fifth infantries became known throughout history as the "buffalo soldiers." The Buffalo Soldiers were just a few of the African Americans who were part of western history.

George Monroe and William Robinson became Pony Express

Bill Pickett was a famous cowboy known for his special bulldogging technique.

riders in California. Bass Reeves was a deputy sheriff in what is now Fort Smith, Arkansas. Clara Brown became a nurse and helper to the people of Colorado. Mary Fields drove a stage-coach in Montana.

Between 5,000 to 8,000 African-American men became cow-boys, wranglers, cooks, and trail bosses. These were hard jobs, but they were plentiful. Many African-American cowboys had served as soldiers during the Civil War and needed jobs after the war was over. They were hired to drive the large herds of cattle in the West to the cattle markets in the North and in the East.

Bill Pickett was an African-American cowboy who also be-came a well-known rodeo star. His most popular rodeo event was steer wrestling or bulldogging a steer. Bill would gallop after the steer and then slide off his horse onto the back of the running animal. Then he would grab a steer by its horns, bite it on its lip, and twist its neck so that it fell over onto the ground. Pickett learned the lip-biting trick from watching cow dogs round up cattle. A fifty-to-sixty-pound dog could hold a cow motionless by biting its lip. Bulldogging is still a popular rodeo event.

African Americans such as Bose Ikard, Daniel "80 John" Wallace, One-Horse Charlie, and Nat "Deadwood Dick" Love became famous cowboys. There were many ways for black peo-ple to make a living in the West.

27

Nat Love (1854–1921)

"Deadwood Dick"

When Nat Love was very young his father died. Although Nat was just a little boy, he had to take care of his family. He became a farmer and also broke in wild horses to make a living. Then,

Nat Love claimed to have won the title of "Deadwood Dick" after a shooting, riding, and roping contest in Deadwood, South Dakota, in 1876.

when he was fourteen years old, Nat won a raffle. He divided the money with his mother and decided to use his share to head out west in 1869.

When Nat arrived in Dodge City, Kansas, he began to look for work as a cowboy. Some cowboys from the Duval Ranch told him that they might have a job for him. They gave Nat a wild bucking bronco to ride as a joke. Little did they know that Nat had been breaking horses for years. When he finally gentled the horse, he was given a job as a cowboy for thirty dollars a month.

Not long after Nat joined the Duval outfit, they were attacked by a band of Indians. When he heard the shouting he quickly learned how to load and shoot a gun. There were many other times that Nat was afraid as a cowboy, but he loved the life on the range. Nat Love became one of the best cowboys in the West.

On July 4, 1876, Nat was visiting the town of Deadwood, South Dakota. The townspeople were holding a competition among the cowboys to see who could rope, throw, tie, bridle, saddle, and mount a wild bronco in the least time. Nat did all of the events in only nine minutes, a record! Next a shooting contest was held, using the Colt .45 at 150 yards and a rifle at 100 and 250 yards. Nat won those contests, too! Soon everyone began calling Nat "Deadwood Dick."

The West began to change. The cowboy and his horse were replaced by the iron horse—railroad tracks soon covered the western prairie. Cattle and other livestock were now shipped by train. Nat knew that the day of the cowboy was coming to an end. He hung up his guns and spurs and got a job as a Pullman porter on a train.

Nat never wanted to forget his life as a cowboy. He wrote a book entitled *The Life and Adventures of Nat Love: Better Known in the Cattle Country as "Deadwood Dick."* He wanted people to know that thousands of black cowboys had roamed the range. Black cowboys played an important part in the settlement of the West.

28

The Exodusters

Henry Adams and Benjamin "Pap" Singleton were part of a group called the Edgefield Real Estate and Homestead Association. Members of this group were tired of the way black

Southern blacks wait for transportation during the Great Migration north in 1879.

people were treated in the South. They traveled across the United States looking for a place where blacks could live in peace. Adams and Singleton wanted to buy property so that black people could start their own towns. They chose Kansas as a good place to live.

Benjamin Singleton printed hundreds of posters and fliers about the peaceful life blacks could have in Kansas. Black people began to leave the South by the thousands. More than twenty thousand blacks left Mississippi, Louisiana, and Texas in the spring of 1879. These people were called "exodusters" because they left the South the same way as, in the biblical Book of Exodus, the Israelites left Egypt for the freedom of the promised land.

29
Going Up North

In 1917 black people made another exodus to the North. World War I had begun. Black men wanted to join the fight to defend democracy. At the beginning of the war, President Woodrow

Wilson refused to allow black men to serve in the combat units of the army, navy, or marines. Finally, after receiving criticism from people all over the country, Wilson allowed the War Department to form the all-black Ninety-second Army Division and other black military units. The black troops received many medals for their bravery during this war. Although this was the war that was fought to "help make the world safe for democracy," black and white soldiers trained, slept, ate, and fought separately.

Men and women were needed to work in the northern factories where war equipment was made. Thousands of black people moved to Detroit, Chicago, and New York. Most blacks were able to earn more in a month "up north" than they had in a year "down south." Because of the great number of men who were in France fighting the war, women were hired as truck drivers, auto mechanics, switchboard operators, elevator operators, ditch diggers, and airplane plant workers. A prosperous new way of life began for many black people "up north."

30
The Harlem Renaissance

The 1920s was an exciting time for black writers, poets, dancers, artists, and musicians. "The New Negro has no fear" was one of the slogans of the time. Harlem, in New York City, was undergoing a rebirth, or "renaissance," during this time because of the many black artists who lived, worked, and performed there. Harlem night spots like the Cotton Club filled the evening air with swinging jazz played by Duke Ellington and Louis "Satchmo" Armstrong. The Roseland Ballroom and the Savoy jumped to the tunes of Fletcher Henderson. The theater productions of *Emperor Jones, Shuffle Along, All God's*

Paul Robeson was a famous football player, singer, actor, and civil rights activist during the Harlem Renaissance.

Chillun Got Wings, Green Pastures, and *Dixie to Broadway* featured black performers such as Paul Robeson, Charles Gilpin, and Florence Mills on stage. Beautiful sculptures by Meta Warwick Fuller, Sargent Johnson, Elizabeth Prophet, Augusta Savage, and Richmond Barthe were on display in Harlem exhibitions. Langston Hughes, Arna Bontemps, Sterling Brown, James Weldon Johnson, Countee Cullen, Claude McKay, Alain Locke, and Zora Neale Hurston wrote books and poems about black history and culture, and the new feeling of pride among black people.

The hardships of the Great Depression, when many people lost their jobs, and the beginning of World War II brought the exciting times of the Harlem Renaissance to an end. But these artists, writers, and entertainers had opened the door for the thousands of creative blacks in the arts and entertainment field today.

31

Zora Neale Hurston (1901?–1960)

Writer, Anthropologist, Folklorist

As a child, Zora Neale Hurston watched the world go by from the fence post in front of her home in Eatonville, Florida. Eatonville was an all-black town, and Zora's father, John, was Eatonville's mayor, minister, and carpenter.

The general store was the heart of the friendly little community. After their work and chores were done, many of Ea-

Zora Neale Hurston's books and folklore collections gave her readers a new view of black life.

tonville's citizens gathered on the porch of the store to visit. Zora loved to listen to the songs, folktales, and "lies" that were swapped in the cool of the evening.

After her mother, Lucy Ann, died and her father remarried, Zora left Eatonville. She joined a traveling show, working as a maid for the actors. She traveled with them for a while, then decided to finish her education, graduating from Morgan College in Baltimore in 1918. She moved to Washington, D.C., and enrolled in Howard University. It was there that her skills as a writer were first discovered. Her short story, "John Redding Goes to Sea," was published in 1921. Soon Zora's short stories, articles, and books were being published around the world. Most of her work, such as her novel *Their Eyes Were Watching God*, is flavored with a spicy dose of the stories she'd heard as a child in Eatonville.

Zora soon became a part of the new generation of black writers and artists who lived and worked in Harlem. She loved to laugh and often told funny stories about Eatonville to her friends Langston Hughes, Alain Locke, and other writers and artists who lived in New York. Zora never forgot the folklore stories and the traditions that surrounded her as a child.

In 1925 Zora received a scholarship from Barnard College in New York to study anthropology under the famous folklorist Franz Boas. Professor Boas taught Zora how to carefully document the stories, folkways, religious customs, and songs of African-American people. Zora returned to her hometown of Eatonville and traveled throughout the South and to Jamaica and Haiti in search of folklore. She would wait patiently until she could become a part of the community and culture she studied. Then she would carefully record the stories, songs, and customs she heard and saw. Her books *Jonah's Gourd Vine*, *Mules and Men*, and *Tell My Horse* contain some of the material she gathered during her travels. Zora made it her lifelong work to preserve and publish the folk culture of African Americans.

She didn't want the wonderful stories and songs she learned to be forgotten.

Because of Zora Neale Hurston's work as an author, anthropologist and folklorist, many of the songs, sayings, and customs, and the folklore humor of African Americans have been preserved.

IV
A MOVEMENT FOR EQUALITY

32

Africa or America?

Many black people felt that the only place they would be able to live in peace and freedom was Africa. Others wanted a separate but equal society for black people in America. Some

Marcus Garvey started the Universal Negro Improvement Association and the "Back to Africa" movement in the 1920s.

groups felt that black people within American society should receive equal treatment and the same respect that other races received.

Marcus Garvey formed the Universal Negro Improvement Association to teach black Americans race pride and independence. He also started a "Back to Africa" movement in the 1920s. Garvey wanted to build a community for American blacks in Monrovia, Liberia, in West Africa. Monrovia was first settled by free blacks and former slaves in 1821, before the Civil War. Garvey's dreams of a strong black nation faded when he was accused of defrauding his followers, imprisoned, and later deported to Jamaica. He was one of the first black leaders to attract a large following among blacks.

Booker T. Washington was the first black principal of Tuskegee Institute in Alabama. Tuskegee Institute was a school for

Booker T. Washington was a powerful politician and the first black principal of Tuskegee Institute in Alabama.

blacks that taught its students the value of hard work, self-help, and independence in business. Washington thought that black people should learn a good trade, open their own businesses, and try to live peaceably among their own people in the South. He felt that blacks would be accepted by whites once they proved themselves and earned their place in society.

W. E. B. Du Bois was an educator, author, and publisher of *Crisis* magazine. Du Bois was against Washington's idea of a society for black people who were only trained for manual labor and menial jobs. He felt that blacks should have the right to occupy any job they were capable of doing and study any subject they wanted to study.

In 1909, on the hundredth anniversary of Abraham Lincoln's birthday, Du Bois and others who were interested in racial equality called together a group of whites and blacks and held

W. E. B. Du Bois was an educator and author, and the publisher of Crisis *magazine.*

The founders of the Niagara Movement, later known as the National Association for the Advancement of Colored People. W. E. B. Du Bois is in the center.

a meeting. The two groups talked about how they could solve some of the problems between whites and blacks in America. Their goal was to work together so that white people and black people could both enjoy the freedom America has to offer. This organization grew into what is now the National Association for the Advancement of Colored People, the NAACP, and it is still in operation today.

In 1896 a Supreme Court case entitled *Plessy* v. *Ferguson* allowed the "equal" separation of whites from blacks in almost every area of American life. Law after law followed that took away more and more rights from black people in America. Black men and women challenged these "separate but equal" or "Jim Crow" laws in court. In 1936 the NAACP hired a young black attorney named Thurgood Marshall to fight in the courts for black equality.

33

Thurgood Marshall (1908–1993)

Civil Rights Attorney, Supreme Court Justice

Thurgood Marshall was in trouble again! His high school teacher decided to punish Thurgood by making him sit in the basement and memorize parts of the United States Constitution. Thurgood seemed to be in trouble quite a bit that year. After making several trips to the basement, he became very familiar with the Constitution of the United States.

Thurgood often had questions about the things he read in the Constitution. There was a part of the Constitution that said everyone should have equal rights. He knew that in America there were equal rights for some, but not for everyone, especially black people.

After graduation, Marshall signed up for predentistry courses at Lincoln University in Pennsylvania. He loved to argue, so he joined the college debate team and spent hours looking up facts and preparing his speeches. After graduation from Lincoln he decided that he liked debating better than dentistry and enrolled at Howard University Law School in Washington, D.C. Professor Charles Houston was teaching an exciting new class in civil rights law. In this class Marshall began to see ways that the "equal rights" he'd read about in the Constitution could be available to everyone.

He spent hours studying the law. He wanted to prove that the "separate but equal" laws in the United States were unjust. He also wanted to be one of the new "social engineers" who were using the law to change things for black people in America.

In 1936 Marshall was hired as a lawyer for the NAACP. He worked with other lawyers in their new civil rights division,

From left, George E. C. Hayes, Thurgood Marshall, and James Nabrit, Jr., celebrate after winning victory in the Supreme Court case Brown v. Board of Education *in 1954.*

traveling around the country defending the rights of black people in court.

Marshall and the other NAACP lawyers worked hard to tear down the "separate but equal" education laws, and the laws that segregated juries, jails, washrooms, restaurants, buses, trolley cars, and soldiers in the armed forces. In 1954 he and the NAACP represented Linda Brown, an elementary school student, and her family before the Supreme Court in their lawsuit to end school segregation in Kansas. The Court ruled that "in the field of education, the doctrine of 'separate but equal' has no place." *Brown* v. *Board of Education* opened the door for many other laws that began to provide equal rights to black Americans.

In another case, nine black students wanted to attend Central High, an all-white high school in Little Rock, Arkansas. The children became known as the "Little Rock Nine." In 1957 Marshall successfully argued for their right to attend Central High. Although Marshall won his case, Governor Orval Faubus and many of the citizens of Little Rock refused to abide by the Court's decision. They heckled the students, spat on them, and threw things at them. President Dwight D. Eisenhower was forced to send an army division to escort the students to and from school.

Thurgood Marshall became known as "Mr. Civil Rights." He won twenty-nine of the thirty-two cases he argued before the Supreme Court, the highest court in America. His work as a civil rights attorney helped black Americans obtain the freedom to vote, sit on juries, purchase property, and attend the school of their choice.

In 1961 President John F. Kennedy appointed Marshall to serve as a judge for the United States Court of Appeals. In 1965 President Johnson appointed him solicitor general of the United States. During his years in office he won many important cases that protected the civil rights of black Americans.

In 1967 President Johnson chose Thurgood Marshall to serve

In 1967 Thurgood Marshall became the first black justice to serve on the United States Supreme Court.

as a justice on the United States Supreme Court. He was the first black person to hold this high office. Marshall served on the Court for twenty-four years and retired from the bench in 1991 at the age of eighty-three. President George Bush selected Clarence Thomas, a black federal appellate court judge who was born in Savannah, Georgia, as his replacement.

As a boy, Thurgood Marshall memorized the Constitution

of the United States and wondered about the freedoms it promised to Americans. As a Supreme Court justice he carefully weighed each case that came before him to ensure that the "equal rights" written about in the Constitution were available to all of America's citizens. Marshall died of heart failure on January 24, 1993.

34
Black Power and Black Pride

By 1960 black people had achieved many things in America. There was a new pride in being black, and in black talent and achievement, along with a revived interest in African and Afro-American history and culture. A natural, or "Afro," hairstyle became very popular among blacks; many black Americans wore African clothing and adopted African names and customs.

Some groups felt their purpose could be achieved nonviolently and through the political system. Other groups carried guns and were ready to fight for their civil rights.

Stokley Carmichael led the Student Nonviolent Coordinating Committee (SNCC); Floyd McKissick formed the Congress of Racial Equality (CORE); Malcolm X was a leader of the Black Muslims; and Huey Newton and Bobby Seale were the founding members of the Black Panther Party. These groups were part of the Black Power movement that swept the country in the 1960s.

Other new organizations focused on uniting black people to gain economic power in the United States. Black people have been successful business owners since the days of slavery. In spite of great difficulties, in the eighteenth century free blacks owned and operated several businesses. One of the most suc-

The Black Panther party was founded by Huey Newton and Bobby Seale in Oakland, California, in 1966. The Panthers marched in protest when Newton was arrested for the murder of an Oakland policeman.

cessful New York City tavern owners in 1770 was a free black man named Samuel Fraunces. Paul Cuffe became the captain of his own ship in 1784 and grew wealthy trading goods with Sierra Leone, West Africa.

After slavery was abolished, several blacks began buying property and setting up businesses that catered personal services to other blacks, such as restaurants; groceries and drugstores; and catering, clothing, construction, and funeral establishments. Annie Turnbo Malone and Madame C. J. Walker became millionaires by manufacturing and marketing hair-care preparations. In 1917 Malone established Poro College, a center that developed beauty products for blacks, one of which was Poro, a line of hair straighteners and oils. The college contained classrooms, laboratories, and a barbershop. Malone trained her assistants in the proper use of Poro products and in a sales

Malcolm X, leader of the Black Muslims, was assassinated on February 21, 1965, while making a speech in New York.

Maggie L. Walker, banker

technique for distributing these products around the country. Madame C. J. Walker, trained by Malone, later established her own business, using some of Malone's techniques. By 1900 there were four black-owned banks, one of which, the Richmond Consolidated Bank and Trust Company in Richmond, Virginia, was directed by a black woman, Maggie L. Walker.

Discrimination hindered the successful growth of many black businesses. Black businessmen and women were unable to secure bank loans and other financial backing necessary for their enterprises to prosper. During the wave of civil rights protests in the late 1960s and 1970s, organizations like People United to Save Humanity (PUSH), headed by Reverend Jesse Jackson, pressured large corporations to support black businesses and to invest in the black community. In 1972, 195,000 black-owned businesses existed. By 1987 there were 424,165 black businesses, with total revenues of some $19 billion. By 1993 blacks owned a variety of successful businesses, ranging from publishing to telecommunications to automobile dealerships and industrial chemical distributors. John H. Johnson, owner of Johnson Publishing Company, founded *Ebony, Jet,* and *EM* magazines. TLC Beatrice International Holdings Inc., a food-processing and distribution company founded by the late Reginald F. Lewis, is one of the most successful black businesses in America. Many members of the black community feel that "black power is green power" and work to achieve financial success in the business world in order to obtain a brighter future for blacks in America.

35

The Civil Rights Movement

Black people wanted the same rights as other Americans. The Thirteenth, Fourteenth, and Fifteenth Amendments to the United States Constitution guaranteed black people their freedom, their citizenship, and the right to vote. However, before 1965, most black people in the South could not vote without passing a test, paying a high tax, or risking their lives. Black children and white children went to separate schools. There were separate bathrooms and water fountains for blacks and whites. A black person could not sit in the front of a bus, try on clothing in a white-owned store, or eat in the same restaurants as whites. In one state even the phone booths were separate for blacks and whites! Most jobs, schools and universities, restaurants, hotels, and recreational places were closed to black people. Black servicemen were sent to fight and die for America in segregated units.

Some black people fought for their rights in court. Others would not use stores, buses, or restaurants that separated blacks and whites. There have been many race riots, marches, demonstrations, and sit-ins to protest unfair treatment of black people in America.

Freedom Riders integrate the Trailways bus station in Montgomery, Alabama, in 1961.

Asa Philip Randolph, leader of the Brotherhood of Sleeping Car Porters, was active in the fight for civil rights.

Black labor organizer A. Philip Randolph fought for better conditions for black men and women in the workplace. In 1941 he made plans for a huge march on Washington to demand that the federal government hire black workers. President Franklin Delano Roosevelt asked him to call off the march, but Randolph refused. President Roosevelt granted Randolph's requests to hire blacks for government jobs and issued Executive Order 8802. The order states: "There shall be no discrimination in the employment of workers in defense industries or Government because of race, creed, color or national origin." Randolph canceled the march.

Many black people felt that equal rights should be won without violence. During the late 1950s and 1960s, Dr. Martin Luther King, Jr., united many black people in the struggle for their civil rights. He believed that black people should protest peacefully, without fighting, to change the laws in America.

The struggle by black people to be respected and treated

fairly was called the civil rights movement. During the civil rights movement, black people protested both peacefully and violently for equal rights under the law.

In 1964 the Civil Rights Bill was signed by President Lyndon Baines Johnson. This new bill promised people of all races equality. America slowly began to change.

36

Dr. Martin Luther King, Jr. (1929–1968)
Coretta Scott King (b. 1927)
Civil Rights Activists

Dr. Martin Luther King, Jr., and his wife, Coretta, were civil rights workers. Martin Luther King, Jr., was born in Atlanta, Georgia, during the time of strict segregation of whites and blacks. Martin's father and his grandfather were Baptist ministers. Every Sunday, for as long as Martin could remember, he listened to them preach at Ebenezer Baptist Church. King was a very good student, and he graduated from high school at the age of fifteen. He wasn't tall, but he had a wonderful, rich baritone voice that made him seem much bigger. He loved to debate and to give speeches. At Morehouse College, King had trouble deciding what he wanted to do in life. He thought about being a lawyer; then he decided to major in sociology and English. Finally, when he was seventeen years old, he decided that he wanted to become a preacher. He preached his first sermon from the same pulpit as his grandfather and his father at Ebenezer Baptist Church.

King wanted to be a minister who helped his congregation. He studied very hard to find ways to end the terrible prejudice he saw all around him in the South. After graduating from Morehouse College, he went to Boston University to work on

Dr. Martin Luther King, Jr., civil rights leader and head of the Southern Christian Leadership Conference

another degree. While he was in Boston, Martin met a beautiful young woman named Coretta Scott.

Coretta Scott was born and raised in Marion, Alabama. In Alabama, as in Georgia, there were separate schools, drinking fountains, entrances, and seating arrangements for whites and blacks. In order to get a high school education, Coretta had to go to school nine miles away in another town, even though there was a school that white children attended not far from her home.

Coretta's parents often told her that she was just as good as anybody else. But all around her were people who told her that because of the color of her skin she was worthless.

Coretta Scott loved to sing and her teachers wanted her to become a concert soloist. She attended Antioch College in Yellow Springs, Ohio. Then Coretta applied for and received a

Coretta Scott King was active in the civil rights movement.

scholarship to the New England Conservatory of Music in Boston. One evening after class Coretta Scott received a phone call from a young man named Martin Luther King. He'd been given Coretta's phone number by a mutual friend. Coretta agreed to meet him for lunch.

On their first date Martin told Coretta that she was everything he had ever wanted in a wife. But she didn't want to be a minister's wife; she wanted to be a concert singer. King was finally able to convince her that helping poor people get good educations and decent jobs was also a special career, and they were married in 1953. Later they moved to Montgomery, Alabama, and Martin Luther King became pastor of Dexter Avenue Baptist Church.

Life would have been very different if the young couple had decided to live in the North. Although the North was not free of racial discrimination, it was better than the South. They wouldn't have had to worry about signs that said *White* and *Colored*, or restaurants that would only let black people eat in the kitchen, if at all, or about having to sit in the back of the bus.

The Montgomery Bus Company boycott was the beginning of Martin Luther King's involvement in the fight for civil rights for black people. Mrs. Rosa Parks, a seamstress and member of the NAACP, had been arrested for not giving up her bus seat to a white man. To protest the bus rules, black people in Mont-

Mrs. Rosa Parks, seamstress and member of the NAACP, was arrested for not giving up her bus seat to a white man.

gomery decided to stop riding the bus until they were treated fairly. For one whole year black people walked and car-pooled— some even used horses and buggies to get to work! Finally, little by little, inch by inch, things began to change. After losing thousands of dollars, the Montgomery Bus Company integrated its buses.

White people and black people, old people and young people from around the United States began to join together in the nonviolent crusade for equal rights. There were sit-ins at restaurants that refused to serve black people, freedom rides to sign up black people who wanted to vote, peace marches, speeches, and rallies.

It was a dangerous time in America. Many people opposed the civil rights workers and their ideas for change. They fought violently against the civil rights movement. Protesters, sit-in participants, and freedom riders were often beaten, sprayed with high-powered water hoses, attacked by dogs, or shot. The Kings' house was bombed, and Martin's life was threatened over and over again. Then on April 4, 1968, Martin Luther King was shot and killed. James Earl Ray was arrested for his murder and is currently serving a life sentence.

Coretta Scott King still believes that white people and black people, rich and poor, can live together in peace. At the Martin Luther King, Jr., Center for Social Change in Atlanta, Georgia, she works to make her husband's dream a reality.

37
Getting Out the Vote

In the 1970s and 1980s black people became more and more involved in politics. The fight for equality through the courts and by voting has become a useful way of bettering the conditions of blacks in America. The number of registered black voters has increased steadily since 1968. From 1970 to 1985 blacks held at least one public office in every state except South Dakota. By 1989 more than 6,800 black men and women held the offices of mayor, state representative, senator, and other elected positions in their states. In 1990 Douglas Wilder of Virginia became the nation's first black governor. That same year Mississippi led the nation with hundreds of black officials and one of the largest numbers of registered black voters in America.

Shirley Chisholm was the first black woman to serve in the U.S. Congress. She served from 1969 to 1982 as a representative from New York. Chisholm was also the first black woman to run for president of the United States. She campaigned very hard for the 1972 Democratic nomination. Chisholm did not

Shirley Chisholm was the first black woman to serve in the U.S. Congress.

win her party's nomination, but she was an inspiration to other black men and women who wanted to become president.

In 1984 and 1988 the Reverend Jesse Jackson ran for the Democratic party's presidential nomination. Jackson made history when he won primaries in ten states, the District of Columbia, Puerto Rico, and the Virgin Islands. He pulled together a strong campaign that involved a "rainbow" of people of all colors and from all walks of life.

During his two campaigns for the presidency Jackson received millions of votes, gained political power, and broke down many of the barriers that had barred blacks from running for president. Although many reasons were given for Jackson's failure to receive the Democratic party's presidential nomination, his race remained a central issue. Jackson decided not to run

During his two campaigns for the U.S. presidency, the Reverend Jesse Jackson received millions of votes.

in the 1992 presidential campaign. He now serves as a "shadow" senator for the District of Columbia.

Blacks continue to make great strides in the world of politics. They have been elected mayors of cities all around the United States. Sharon Pratt Dixon became the first African-American woman mayor of Washington, D. C., in 1990. Two of the largest cities in America have elected black mayors: David Dinkins, mayor of New York City; and Tom Bradley, mayor of Los Angeles. In 1992 Carol Moseley-Braun from Illinois became the first black woman to be elected to the U.S. Senate. A total of forty black lawmakers held office in the Congress and Senate in 1992.

Upon his election as president, Bill Clinton appointed a number of African Americans to serve in his cabinet and to other positions in his administration. Clinton named Ron Brown, former chairman of the Democratic National Committee, secretary of commerce; former Mississippi representative Michael Espy secretary of agriculture; Hazel O'Leary secretary of energy; and Jesse Brown secretary of veterans' affairs.

Black politicians have united people of all races to work together to improve their cities and states. They have created many programs that have benefited people from all walks of life, from drug-rehabilitation programs to better housing. These politicians have helped to make the American political system work for all Americans.

V
BREAKING DOWN
THE BARRIERS

38
Marching Through History

Black men and women have been active in the defense of America since the earliest times. Blacks have held positions of rank in all branches of the military and have been awarded every medal of distinction given for valor and service in the armed forces.

For many years black servicemen and -women bravely endured the terrors of battle, along with mistreatment by the very country they have risked their lives to defend. Military units were racially segregated and black military personnel were not allowed to train, eat, or share housing with whites. There were very few black officers, and they were seldom given the respect or privileges accorded to white officers of the same rank. Often blacks were given assignments doing menial labor or were placed in the most dangerous front line positions during battle. Even with all these hardships, black men and women have an outstanding record of service in the military.

During the Spanish-American War of 1898, Private T. C. Butler of the Twenty-fifth Infantry, Sergeant Major Edward L. Baker, and six others were awarded the Medal of Honor for their bravery in combat at El Caney, Santiago, and San Juan Hill.

During World War I the Fighting 369th, an all-black unit, remained on the French front lines nonstop for 191 days in 1918 without losing a trench, retreating an inch, or surrendering one prisoner. Privates Henry Johnson and Needham Roberts and the other members of the unit were given the Croix de Guerre by the French government, one of that country's highest awards, for their bravery.

Colonel Benjamin O. Davis, Jr., whose father, Benjamin O. Davis, Sr., became America's first black general in 1940, commanded the Ninety-ninth Pursuit Squadron during World War II. This squadron, an all-black unit of fighter pilots, was also known as the Fighting Redtails because of the red markings on its planes. By 1945 this unit, along with the black 332nd Fighter Group, had engaged in over 1,600 combat missions. The Fighting Redtails became one of the most successful black fighting units of World War II. A black sailor, Dorie Miller, also became famous during World War II when he downed four Japanese planes as they attacked Pearl Harbor on December 7, 1941.

American military units were integrated for the first time during the Korean War. Many all-black units were replaced or expanded to include white soldiers. General Daniel "Chappie" James became an ace pilot during this war and was the first black four-star general.

After the Korean War ended, and before the war in Vietnam began, President John F. Kennedy attempted to better the conditions of black enlisted personnel in the military, both on and off base. However, the same racial conflicts that separated black and white civilians, separated black and white military personnel.

Many changes have occurred in the military since the first integrated units fought together in the Korean War. The military is now operated on a volunteer basis. More and more young black men and women are enlisting in the service to escape unemployment and to take advantage of the educational benefits the military has to offer.

A record number of black servicemen and -women were

involved in the Persian Gulf conflict, Operation Desert Storm. Many members of the black community were alarmed by the large number of blacks who served on the front lines during this conflict and addressed their complaints to Washington. Their complaints were reviewed by the highest-ranking military officer, General Colin Powell, the first black chairman of the Joint Chiefs of Staff.

39

General Colin Luther Powell (b. 1937)

Chairman, Joint Chiefs of Staff

General Colin Luther Powell grew up in a tough Harlem neighborhood in New York City. His mother and father were Jamaican immigrants who tried to do the best that they could for their son. His mother worked as a seamstress and his father worked as a foreman in a garment factory. School was a struggle for Powell. He was placed in the "slow" class in the fifth grade and was a C student in high school. Powell's grades were not very good, but he loved books and reading. A natural leader, he was elected captain of his graduating class at Morris High School.

After graduation Powell decided to attend the City College of New York. One of Powell's classes was the Reserve Officers' Training Corps (ROTC). This course prepared students for a career in the military. Powell received an A in this class. He also earned the highest possible rank, Cadet Colonel.

Powell joined the army after graduation as a second lieutenant. At first, he thought that he would just stay in for two years. It was a way to escape the poverty and violence of Harlem, and it would give him a chance to travel. Good jobs were hard to find in Harlem, and the army paid fairly well.

General Colin Luther Powell, first black chairman of the U.S. Joint Chiefs of Staff

Powell found he enjoyed the military, and he received higher and higher ranks. He commanded an infantry battalion in South Korea and served two tours of duty in Vietnam, where he won eleven medals, including the Bronze Star for the rescue of four men from a burning helicopter, and the Purple Heart.

After the war Powell decided to further his education. He attended George Washington University, where he received his master's degree in business administration. He was also selected as a White House Fellow in the Office of Management and Budget. This program gave him an opportunity to work with senators, representatives, and other officials in Washington and to learn firsthand how government works. He also met people who would be important to his career, such as Caspar Weinberger, director of the Office of Management and Budget and later the secretary of defense, and Frank Carlucci, associate director of the Office of Management and Budget.

When Carlucci became the national security adviser he chose Powell as his deputy. When Carlucci became secretary of defense Powell was his choice to become the first black chairman of the Joint Chiefs of Staff.

As chairman, Powell became the highest-ranking officer in the military. He played key roles in decisions about the invasion of Panama and in military maneuvers taking place during Operation Desert Storm. Powell's job is to make sure that America is secure and safe, and that our military is ready to defend our country. The lives of thousands of soldiers depend on his decisions.

40

Running Down Racism

Blacks have successfully competed in every major sporting event from auto racing to wrestling. But the same laws of segregation and racial discrimination that black people faced in other areas of society also appeared in the world of sports.

Before 1950, the lack of funds and facilities excluded many blacks from competing in sports that required expensive equipment or long years of training. Until then, most sporting events were segregated and black athletes were not allowed to compete against whites. School athletic programs gave black athletes an opportunity to train and to compete in the sports offered there, such as baseball, basketball, boxing, football, and track. Even though most black athletes were handicapped by racial discrimination, blacks still achieved significant records in all areas of sports.

Isaac Murphy began his career as a jockey after the Civil War. He was so good that he seldom used a whip on his horses. He won the Kentucky Derby three times and was known as one of America's greatest jockeys. In all, he rode in 1,412 races and won 628 of them.

From the early 1800s until around 1905, black jockeys such as William "Billy" Walker, Willie Simms, "Soup" Perkins, Jimmy Lee, and Jimmy Winkfield won race after race. They earned hundreds of thousands of dollars in prize money for their sponsors. However, the Jockey Club, which was organized in 1894 to license all riders, refused to issue licenses to blacks. Even the successful black jockeys were forced out of horse racing, and, until recently, very few blacks have participated in this sport.

In 1898 Marshall "Major" Taylor overcame extreme racial barriers to become the first native-born African American to win a national cycling title. Taylor won many races and set countless records during his sixteen years as a professional racer.

On July 4, 1910, Jack Johnson became the first black boxer ever to compete against a white champion for the heavyweight boxing title. After a fifteen-round fight, Johnson knocked James Jeffries to the canvas and became the undisputed heavyweight champion of the world! Since that great victory, heavyweight boxing has been dominated by black titleholders such as Joe Louis, Muhammad Ali, George Foreman, Larry Holmes, Mike Tyson, and Evander Holyfield.

Around 1920 black sporting leagues were formed. Andrew "Rube" Foster, an outstanding pitcher with the all-black Cuban Giants, has been called "The Father of Negro Baseball." In 1919 Foster called a meeting of all the heads of the black baseball leagues. At that meeting the Negro National League was formed and Foster was elected president. For the first time, black baseball teams had set schedules. Rules and regulations were developed and players' salaries were increased. Foster's

Jack Johnson (left) *became the world's first black heavyweight boxing champion in 1908. He held the title for seven years.*

organizational genius and playing strategies made black baseball games sporting events that drew thousands of fans. Many fine black baseball players, such as Cristobal Torriente, Jimmy Lyons, Josh Gibson, Satchel Paige, Jelly Gardner, "Bingo" DeMoss, Dave Malarcher, "Smokey Joe" Williams, and Grant "Home Run" Johnson, had spectacular careers in the Negro leagues. Unfortunately, most of the outstanding baseball players in the Negro leagues never received the wealth or fame that was awarded to the white players of their day.

Jesse Owens won four gold medals during the 1936 Olympics.

One of the greatest moments in the Olympics happened in 1936. Jesse Owens, a track star from Ohio State University, used his warm personality and natural athletic abilities to prove an important point during those games. The 1936 Olympics were held in Nazi Germany. Adolf Hitler, the Nazi leader, believed in white supremacy and was sure that no black man could beat his "master race" of white athletes. Jesse Owens proved Hitler wrong by winning four gold medals in the track-and-field events. Hitler left the games in an embarrassed huff. Jesse left a set of world records that stood for decades. Wilma Rudolph,

In 1947 Jackie Robinson became the first black player to sign with the major leagues.

Rafer Johnson, Florence Griffith Joyner, Jackie Joyner-Kersee, Edwin Moses, Carl Lewis, and Evelyn Ashford followed the trail blazed by Jesse Owens in Olympic track-and-field events.

In 1947 Jackie Robinson signed with the Brooklyn Dodgers. He became the first black to play in the major leagues. Robinson endured mountains of abuse from people who didn't want him to play for the all-white team. His willingness to take a stand and his wonderful athletic skills helped to break down many of the color barriers in professional baseball for outstanding players like Roy Campanella, Roberto Clemente, Willie Mays,

Tennis star Althea Gibson won the French Championships in 1957, Wimbledon in 1957, and the U.S. Nationals in 1958.

Frank Robinson, Hank Aaron, Reggie Jackson, Maury Wills, Lou Brock, and Rickey Henderson.

Althea Gibson's lightning strokes on the courts of the West Side Tennis Club opened up the doors of competitive tennis for other black tennis players such as Arthur Ashe, Lori McNeil, and Zina Garrison. After a long, hard struggle, Gibson won the

French Championships in 1957, Wimbledon in 1957, and the U.S. Nationals in 1958. Gibson became the first black superstar of tennis.

Many black soldiers returning from World War II took advantage of the opportunity to attend college on the G.I. Bill. Some of these men became outstanding football players. Black college athletes played football with their white teammates in game after game, although few, if any, were allowed to live in the campus dormitories. Wally Triplett and Denny Hoggard became the first black athletes to play football at the Cotton Bowl. Triplett and Hoggard played for Penn State against Southern Methodist University on New Year's Day, 1948. The game ended up tied 13–13, but Triplett and Hoggard won a small victory for black college athletes, who had often been barred from playing against whites.

Roosevelt Brown, Charles Brackins, Willie McClung, Paul Younger, and Willie Davis played football for black colleges such as Morgan State, Prairie View A&M, Grambling, and Florida A&M. These men later became the first black college athletes to sign with the National Football League.

Bill Russell and other black college athletes such as Wilt Chamberlin, K. C. Jones, Kareem Abdul-Jabbar, and Spencer Haywood transferred their college success into contracts with professional basketball leagues. By the 1980s black players dominated basketball. In 1981 Earvin "Magic" Johnson became one of the highest paid basketball players in history when he signed a contract for $25 million with the Los Angeles Lakers. Michael Jordan also became wealthy, as a basketball star and through his endorsement of a number of commercial products from cereal to tennis shoes.

Black athletes of the past had to compete against racism before they could play the sport of their choice. Their sacrifices paved the way for black men and women in the world of sports today.

41

Old Barriers, New Discoveries

Each time you sharpen a pencil, mow your lawn, use an ironing board, or stop at a traffic light you're using one of the hundreds of inventions patented by black inventors and scientists. Blacks have been designing and building their inventions throughout history. Many items developed by black inventors are in wide use today.

For many years blacks were not allowed to receive patents for their inventions. A patent gives a person the sole right to produce, sell, and profit from his or her invention. Often blacks were forced to have their inventions patented by whites. Many of these inventors never received any recognition for their invention or profits from its sale.

Black men and women created hundreds of inventions before 1900. Benjamin Banneker, a mathematician, surveyor, and astronomer, invented the first accurate American-made wooden clock in 1753. Norbert Rillieux of New Orleans created a sugar-refining process that changed the sugar industry in 1846. Lewis H. Latimer worked as a special assistant to Thomas Alva Edison and created the incandescent electric light bulb with a carbon filament in 1881. Jan Matzeliger's creation of a special machine for making shoes in 1883 cut manufacturing time to a minute and the price of shoes in half. Sarah Boone invented the ironing board in 1892. Dr. Daniel Hale Williams, a medical scientist, performed the first open-heart surgery in 1893. J. L. Love invented the pencil sharpener in 1897.

Garrett A. Morgan's numerous inventions helped to ease some of the problems of a modern world. In 1914 he received a patent for his Safety Hood, which was the first type of gas mask. Morgan and his brother Frank used the Safety Hood to rescue a group of men who were trapped in a tunnel after an explosion.

Norbert Rillieux of New Orleans. His invention of the evaporating pan in 1846 changed the sugar industry.

Garrett A. Morgan developed the first gas mask and the first stoplight, and designed twenty-two other inventions.

99

Morgan also created the first traffic signal, which was patented in November 1923. One day Morgan saw a terrible accident involving a horse and carriage and an automobile at a street intersection. The driver of the car was knocked unconscious, the passengers in the carriage were thrown into the street, and the horse had to be shot. Morgan thought about a way to solve this problem. He built an electric signal with lights of different colors for stop and go. Morgan later sold his traffic signal to the General Electric Corporation. He also held patents for twenty-two other inventions.

Granville T. Woods, an engineer, developed countless inventions, from the railway telegraph to the egg incubator. Most of his designs serve as patterns for modern devices.

Dr. George Washington Carver developed hundreds of products—from butter to paint—using peanuts, sweet potatoes, and soybeans.

Dr. George Washington Carver developed hundreds of products—from butter to paint—from peanuts, sweet potatoes, and soybeans. His experiments created new cash crops for southern agriculture and new sources of income for the South.

Dr. Charles Drew discovered in 1940 that liquid blood plasma without its red and white cells could be stored for long periods of time. This saved thousands of lives and started the first blood banks.

Dr. Percy Julian, a chemist, held more than eighty-six patents. His research on drugs, such as cortisone, which was perfected in 1950, has led to medicines that provide relief for many who suffer from crippling arthritis and skin diseases. His development of physostigmine has helped save the eyesight of thousands of people who face blindness from glaucoma.

Research and inventions by black scientists have played a great part in America's space program. Dr. Robert E. Shurney developed some of the special equipment used by the astronauts during the Skylab spaceship mission in 1970. He created metal chevrons for the wheels of the moon buggy that was used to explore the moon's surface. The metal chevrons kept the moon dust away from the astronauts as they traveled. George Carruthers works as an astrophysicist with the National Aeronautics and Space Administration (NASA). He developed the Far Ultraviolet Camera, which was used to take photographs during the Apollo 16 flight. Discoveries by black inventors and scientists continue to improve life for all humankind on earth and in space.

Black women are entering the field of science in greater numbers. Dr. Jennie Patrick was the first black woman in the United States to receive a Ph.D. in chemical engineering. Dr. Shirley A. Jackson's physics research for AT&T Bell Laboratories has won praise from around the world. Dr. Mae C. Jemison, M.D., was selected by NASA as the first black woman candidate to become an astronaut.

42

Dr. Mae C. Jemison (b. 1956)

One lucky June day Dr. Mae C. Jemison received the news she'd been waiting for. She had been selected as the first black woman to enter the NASA training program!

Dr. Jemison was born in Decatur, Alabama, but soon moved to Chicago, Illinois, with her parents, Charlie and Dorothy Jemison. After finishing a dual degree in chemical engineering and African and Afro-American studies, Jemison decided on a career as a doctor. She completed her medical studies at Cornell University and her medical internship in 1982. Then Jemison signed up with the Peace Corps as a medical officer. She was assigned to Sierra Leone and Liberia in West Africa. For the

Dr. Mae C. Jemison, M.D., was selected by NASA as the first black woman candidate to become an astronaut.

first time, Jemison was able to travel to the place she'd studied about for so long, Africa!

For three years Jemison worked to improve the health conditions of the people in Sierra Leone and Liberia. When she returned to the United States, Jemison moved to California to open a medical practice, where she also became interested in the space program. Many exciting things were happening at the Lyndon B. Johnson Space Center in Houston, Texas. Black men such as Guion Bluford, Frederick Gregory, Charles F. Bolden, Jr., and Ronald McNair had been accepted as NASA astronaut candidates. But no black women were a part of the program.

Jemison applied to the NASA program and also began taking graduate engineering classes. When she received the exciting news that she had been chosen as one of the fifteen astronaut candidates out of the two thousand who had applied, Jemison moved from California to Houston to begin her training.

Jemison completed the difficult one-year candidate training course in August 1988, which qualified her to serve as a mission specialist on the Space Shuttle flight crew. She was assigned to Spacelab-J, a cooperative mission between the United States and Japan.

On September 12, 1992, Jemison boarded the Endeavor Space Shuttle and became the first black woman in space. Jemison, who loves to dance, took along an Alvin Ailey American Dance Theater poster.

During her six-week-long orbit around the earth, Jemison studied the effects of motion sickness and how it can be avoided. Unlike the other six crew members, Jemison did not take medicine to avoid the nausea that astronauts sometimes experience while in space. Instead, she used positive thinking, relaxation techniques, and meditation as ways to combat sickness.

Jemison also conducted fertilization experiments with a group of pregnant frogs to see if gravity had any effect on their tadpoles' development. Both of her experiments were successful. She didn't get motion sickness, and the tadpoles hatched into healthy frogs. While in space, Jemison conducted a live telecast to the Museum of Science and Industry in her hometown of Chicago. Someone asked her how she felt. "I'm closer to the stars," Jemison said. "Somewhere I've always wanted to be."

43
Color and Creativity

Black creativity in all areas of the arts from music to murals has had a great influence on American culture. African slaves wove their native songs and chants, gospel songs, and musical rhythms into American music. In 1899 Scott Joplin, a black composer, created "Maple Leaf Rag" and other popular ragtime tunes and soon became known as the "King of the Ragtime Writers." Many of his songs are still played today.

In 1899 Scott Joplin, a black composer, created "Maple Leaf Rag" and other popular ragtime tunes and soon became known as the "King of the Ragtime Writers."

Duke Ellington was a composer, musician, and bandleader.

From 1920 through the 1940s black rhythm and blues, swing, and jazz music became very popular and spread around the world. Jazz is a form of music that was created by black Americans. It is a combination of African drum rhythms, work songs from slavery, and gospel hymns, with a little European and ragtime music mixed in its 4/4 beat.

Saxophonists Sidney Bechet and Coleman Hawkins, trumpeters Joe "King" Oliver and Louis Armstrong, and the big bands led by Duke Ellington and Count Basie were the early pioneers of the jazz sound. Ellington, Basie, and Lionel Hampton were highly successful "big band" leaders, while Bechet, Oliver, and Armstrong concentrated on New Orleans-style jazz. Although these sounds remained popular, new kinds of jazz were born. Charlie Parker, "Dizzy" Gillespie, and John Coltrane

James Baldwin's books and plays revealed the emotions of modern African Americans.

played "Be-bop" in the 1940s. Some musicians were identified with one particular style, but others—like Miles Davis—bridged several types, starting with Be-bop in the 1950s and moving on to "cool" and "fusion" jazz in the 1960s and 1970s. Jazz musicians include Coleman Hawkins, Ray Charles, Herbie Hancock, Wynton Marsalis, and Branford Marsalis. Not all of these performers have limited themselves to jazz, however; Ray Charles plays a mixture of jazz, blues, and contemporary music. Wynton Marsalis, a trumpeter, also has had a very successful career in classical music; he and his brother Branford, who plays tenor and soprano saxophone, are two young African Americans who have continued the musical tradition of jazz into the 1990s.

Rock and roll burst onto the musical scene in the 1950s and

1960s. Many white musicians patterned their musical styles after the swinging, foot-stomping performances of black artists such as Chuck Berry, Little Richard, and James Brown.

Reggae, soul music, and the hip-hop sound of rap have also had a great influence on American music. Bob Marley, a native of Jamaica, introduced reggae music to America. Prince, Michael Jackson, Janet Jackson, and Whitney Houston have had hit after hit on the record charts and have made millions of dollars in the music industry. Hammer, Arrested Development, TLC, Naughty by Nature, and Kris Kross, changed rap from an inner-city style of music and dress to an international sound form.

Theater, television, and movies were slow to provide accurate views of black life. But now, black actors and actresses, formerly given minor roles, are playing major roles in every part of the production process, from writing to performing.

The play A Raisin in the Sun, *written by Lorraine Hansberry, was one of the first Broadway productions written, directed, and acted by blacks.*

During the 1960s black playwrights such as Lorraine Hansberry, James Baldwin, Imamu Amiri Baraka, Lonne Elder, and Charles Gordone wrote thought-provoking plays such as *A Raisin in the Sun, The Amen Corner, Blues for Mister Charlie, Dutchman, Ceremonies in Dark Old Men,* and *No Place to Be Somebody,* which were presented on and off Broadway. Playwright August Wilson has won Pulitzer Prizes for his plays *Fences* and *The Piano Lesson* and a number of other awards for his plays *Ma Rainey's Black Bottom, Joe Turner's Come and Gone,* and *Two Trains Running.* Charles Fuller's work, *A Soldier's Play,* also a Pulitzer Prize winner, was performed by the award-winning Negro Ensemble Company, and later was produced as the movie *A Soldier's Story.* These plays bring a realistic picture of black life to the theater.

Blacks have gained power behind the scenes in the television industry. Jennifer Lawson is chief programmer for the Public Broadcasting Service (PBS). Black producers and directors like

*In 1968 Gordon Parks became the first black man to direct a film (*The Learning Tree*) for a major studio. His photographs have documented many aspects of African-American life.*

Thomas Carter, Debbie Allen, and Michael Moye provide television with programs that reflect black life and culture. Actor Bill Cosby, talk show hosts Oprah Winfrey and Arsenio Hall, and news anchors Bryant Gumbel, Bernard Shaw, and Charlayne Hunter-Gault are well-known television personalities.

Oscar Micheaux's film *The Homesteader*, which was produced in 1918, was the first film directed by a black. In 1968 Gordon Parks became the first black man to direct a film (*The Learning Tree*) for a major studio. Sidney Poitier and Melvin Van Peebles also produced many black films in the 1970s. Robert Townsend, Mario Van Peebles, Spike Lee, Charles Lane, John Singleton,

Katherine Dunham traveled to the Caribbean and Brazil to study native dances. She has been called "the mother of Afro-American dance."

and Warren and Reginald Hudlin form a new league of black filmmakers. Their films *Hollywood Shuffle, New Jack City, Malcolm X, True Identity, Boyz N the Hood,* and *House Party* show black life from many different perspectives. Poet Laureate Maya Angelou's film *Georgia, Georgia* was the first to be directed by a black woman. Other black women such as Euzham Palcy and Julie Dash have also directed major films.

Black men and women have greatly influenced American dance. Katherine Dunham traveled to the Caribbean and Brazil to study primitive dances. She started her own dance group, the Dunham Company, in the 1930s. Dunham blended the native dance steps she'd learned with modern movements. She has been called the "mother of Afro-American dance." Black dance troupes formed by Arthur Mitchell and Alvin Ailey combined African-American dance steps with traditional European dance forms. Their influence proved that black dancers could master intricate steps of classical ballet while creating an exciting new dance style. Debbie Allen and Judith Jamison carry on the black dance tradition with performances on television and the stage and in the movies.

The rich voices of Marian Anderson and Leontyne Price opened up the world of opera to the current group of black divas, stars of the opera world. Jessye Norman, Barbara Hendricks, Kathleen Battle, Leona Mitchell, Isola Jones, Roberta Alexander, and Harolyn Blackwell are a few of the black women whose beautiful voices have brought new excitement to opera. More black men have obtained starring roles in operas, too. Tenors Steven Cole, Vincent Cole, Philip Creech, and George Shirley; baritones Andrew Smith, Arthur Thompson, Robert McFerrin, and Ben Holt; and bass-baritone Simon Estes have successfully appeared in a variety of operas.

Since the time of slavery, black artists have presented a vivid picture of African-American life for the whole world to view. Scipio Morehead, John James Audubon, Edward Mitchell Ban-

The rich voices of Marian Anderson (above) *and Leontyne Price* (left) *opened up the world of opera to the current group of black divas, stars of the opera world.*

nister, Joshua Johnston, Patrick Reason, Henry Ossawa Tanner, Edmonia Lewis, and Horace Pippin were early black artists. Many works by these artists have been preserved and are on display in galleries around the world.

Tina Allen's sculptures are seen in museums and as part of the sets on many popular television shows. A copy of sculptress Selma Burke's bust of Franklin Delano Roosevelt appears on every dime. The paintings of David Hammons and Synthia St. James reflect the African-American experience. Jacob Lawrence, who is one of the most famous black artists in the world, has painted the American scene for more than fifty years.

44

Jacob Lawrence (b. 1917)

Rosealee Lawrence was worried about her young son, Jacob. She was afraid that he would get into trouble while she was at work. Mrs. Lawrence decided to register Jacob in a special after-school program that was held at Utopia House. Utopia House offered classes for children in a variety of subjects. Jacob decided to attend the art classes and found that he had a special talent for drawing and painting.

Lawrence grew up in Harlem during the Great Depression, at the close of the Harlem Renaissance. "The thirties were actually a wonderful period in Harlem although we didn't know this at the time," he says. "Of course, it wasn't wonderful for our parents. For them, it was a struggle, but for the younger people coming along like myself, there was a real vitality in the community."

Lawrence's bright, bold paintings of Harlem life reflect the bittersweet black experience and the strong sense of community in Harlem during his youth. "I had acceptance at a very early

*Augusta Savage,
sculptress and teacher,
helped many young
black artists during the
Harlem Renaissance.*

age from the community, and that does a lot," he says. "The people that accepted me didn't necessarily know about art, but they encouraged me. I got most of my encouragement from Charles Alston and Augusta Savage."

Alston, an artist and director of the Works Progress Administration (WPA) Harlem Art Workshop, which was located in his studio at 306 West 141st Street, and Savage, a sculptress and teacher, were enthusiastic in their support of Lawrence and his work. "At '306' I came in contact with so many older people in other fields of art," says Lawrence. "Claude McKay, Countee Cullen, dancers, . . . musicians. Socially, that was my whole life at that time, the '306' Studio." Many other members of the Harlem community made a lasting impression on Lawrence. "Professor" Seyfert, a carpenter by trade and a scholar and teacher of black history by choice, regularly held classes and lectured on black history and culture. Lawrence often attended

Jacob Lawrence, one of the most famous black artists in the world, has painted the American scene for more than fifty years.

Seyfert's lectures. "One of his projects," says Lawrence, "(besides the collecting of books pertaining to black history) was to get black artists and young people such as myself who were interested in art . . . to select as our content black history. For me, and for a few others, Seyfert was a most inspiring and exciting man in that he helped to give us something that we needed at that time."

Lawrence has depicted black history's heroes and heroines in his multipaneled paintings of the lives of Toussaint-L'Ouverture, Frederick Douglass, Harriet Tubman, George Washington Carver, and John Brown. The paintings are done in a story series, and each panel has a narrative caption written by Lawrence and his wife, Gwen.

In 1941 Edith Halpert, the owner of the Downtown Gallery

in New York, agreed to represent Lawrence. It was the first time a major New York gallery had ever presented the work of a black artist. Halpert organized an exhibition entitled "American Negro Art: 19th and 20th Centuries," which featured Lawrence's sixty-panel work *Migration of the Negro.*

Fortune magazine reproduced twenty-six paintings of the series along with an article on the plight of black people in America. Halpert's guidance and the article about his work in *Fortune* provided Jacob Lawrence with nationwide attention.

Lawrence has never forgotten his Harlem heritage. He has the special ability to use brilliant tempera paints to express the things every race has in common—love, hate, death, food, family, hope, joy, and despair. "My pictures express my life and experience," says Lawrence. "I paint the things I know about and the things I have experienced extend into my national, racial, and class group. So I paint the American scene."

Lawrence is an NAACP Spingarn Medal winner, a member of the American Academy of Arts and Letters, an author, and a teacher and lecturer. His paintings are in many major art galleries and frequently tour across the United States.

45

Black People Today

From the time the first group of African captives arrived in Jamestown in 1619 until today, black people have shaped America's history in a special way. As explorers, inventors, astronauts, ballerinas, jockeys, scientists, writers, fighters, bankers, musicians, doctors, lawyers and politicians, artists, mathematicians, and actors, black people have been and can be anything they want to be. Black people have and continue to hold an important place in history.

IMPORTANT DATES IN AFRICAN-AMERICAN HISTORY

1492
*Pedro Alonso Niño arrives with Columbus. African slaves also explore with Núñez de Balboa, Ponce de León, Cortés, Pizarro, and Menéndez de Avilés.

1501
*Spain allows the use of African slaves in the New World.

1526
*African slaves escape from the first settlement in America (established by Spain in Florida and South Carolina) and go to live with the Indians.

1538
*Estevanito (Little Stephen), a guide for Spanish explorers, leads an expedition from Mexico. Estevanito traveled in what is now Arizona and New Mexico.

1600
*Over nine hundred thousand Africans are enslaved in Latin America by 1600.

1619

*Twenty Africans on board a Dutch vessel are bartered as indentured servants in exchange for food to the colonists at Jamestown, Virginia. The Africans probably serve for seven years and then are given their freedom.

1639

*Captain William Pierce, a New England seaman, sails to the West Indies and exchanges Indian slaves for Africans.

1640

*The sugar industry grows in the West Indies. For the next ten years slavery increases to keep up with the demand. By 1645 there are six thousand slaves in Barbados.

1641

*Massachusetts legalizes slavery, the first colony in America to do so.

1663

*A house servant informs slave owners about an uprising planned by slaves and white indentured servants in Gloucester, Virginia.

*Maryland passes a law that gives all imported Africans the status of slaves.

1672

*Virginia law gives rewards for the capture of "Maroons," runaway slaves. Maroons hid in the mountains, swamps, and forests and often attacked towns and plantations.

1688

*Quakers sign a petition protesting slavery. This was the first formal protest against slavery in America.

1696

*Quakers who import slaves are threatened with expulsion from the Quaker Society.

1727

*The Junto, an organization founded in Philadelphia by Benjamin Franklin, opposes slavery.

1739

*Cato, a slave, leads a violent slave revolt in South Carolina.

1746

*Lucy Terry, a slave, writes "Bars Fight," about the Deerfield Massacre. Terry is thought to be the first African-American poet.

1754

*Twenty-two-year-old Benjamin Banneker, a free African American and a mathematician, gazetteer, astronomer, and inventor, builds the first wooden clock in North America. For more than twenty years the clock accurately chimes the hour.

1769

*Thomas Jefferson fails in his efforts to pass a bill in the Virginia House of Burgesses that would free the slaves.

1770

*Crispus Attucks is shot and killed during the Boston Massacre.

1773

Poems on Various Subjects, Religious and Moral, written by poet Phillis Wheatley, is published. This is the first book published by an African American and the second book published by an American woman.

1775

*The first abolitionist society in America is organized in Philadelphia.

*Salem Poor, Peter Salem, and other African Americans fight at Bunker Hill.

1776

* The Declaration of Independence is adopted. The section written by Thomas Jefferson about the injustice of slavery is removed from the final document.

*George Washington crosses the Delaware River to attack the British in Trenton, New Jersey. Two African-American soldiers, Prince Whipple and Oliver Cromwell, cross the Delaware with Washington.

1778

*A regiment of three hundred slaves is formed in Rhode Island. The men are promised their freedom after the end of the revolutionary war.

1781

*African-American soldiers fight against Cornwallis at Yorktown.

1782

*Deborah Gannet, an African-American woman, disguises herself as a man and joins the Fourth Massachusetts Regiment. Gannet is given a citation for her bravery.

1783

*The revolutionary war is over. More than ten thousand African Americans served in the Continental Army.

1787

*African-American preachers Richard Allen and Absalom Jones organize the Free African Society in Philadelphia.

*Congress passes the Northwest Ordinance, which bans the spread of slavery into the Northwest Territory.

*The New York Manumission Society opens the African Free School in New York City.

1790

*Jean Baptiste Point Du Sable, whose mother was an African slave, starts the first permanent settlement in what is now Chicago.

1791

*Toussaint-L'Ouverture leads slaves in a revolt that becomes the start of the Haitian Revolution.

*Thomas Jefferson recommends that Benjamin Banneker be appointed to the commission organized to lay out the plans for the city of Washington.

1793

*The Fugitive Slave Act is passed in Philadelphia. This law makes it a crime to hide a slave or prevent his arrest.

*Eli Whitney patents the cotton gin. Profits from growing cotton and the demand for slave labor are greatly increased.

1800

*Gabriel Prosser's plan to lead thousands of slaves in a revolt in Richmond, Virginia, is discovered. Prosser and fifteen others are later hanged.

1804

*By this date, slavery has been abolished in most of the northern states (Vermont, Massachusetts, New Hampshire, Pennsylvania, Connecticut, Rhode Island, New York, and New Jersey) or laws are in effect for its gradual elimination.

1808

*A law banning the importation of any new slaves into America takes effect as of January 1. This law is seldom enforced.

1811

*Paul Cuffee, a wealthy African-American shipbuilder, sails with a small group of African Americans to Sierra Leone, West Africa, to start an independent community there.

*Slaves led by Charles Deslands revolt in Louisiana. More than one hundred slaves are killed or executed.

1812

*Free African Americans fight in the War of 1812.

1814

*African-American sailors fight with Oliver Hazard Perry and Isaac Chauncey during the War of 1812. Two battalions of African-American soldiers, many led by African-American officers, help Andrew Jackson defeat the British at the Battle of New Orleans.

1816

*Richard Allen is elected bishop of the newly organized African Methodist Episcopal Church in Philadelphia.

*African-American explorer James P. Beckwourth signs on as a scout with William Henry Ashley's Rocky Mountain expedition.

*The American Colonization Society is formed to send free African Americans back to Africa.

1817

*Philadelphia African Americans hold protest meetings against the American Colonization Society.

*Frederick Douglass, abolitionist, journalist, and statesman, is born in Tuckhoe, Maryland.

1818

*A band of runaway slaves and Creek Indians is defeated during the Battle of Suwanee by an army unit in Fort Blount, Florida. This leads to the end of the first Seminole war.

1820

*Congress votes to enact the Missouri Compromise. Missouri enters the Union as a slave state, Maine as a free state. There are twelve free and twelve slave states as of this date. The compromise forbids slavery north of the southern boundary of Missouri.

*Eighty-six African Americans sail from New York to Sierra Leone, West Africa, on the *Mayflower of Liberia*.

1822

*Denmark Vesey is betrayed, arrested, and hung, along with thirty-six others, for planning a slave revolt.

1823

*Mississippi passes a law that forbids meetings of more than five slave or free African Americans. Teaching slaves to read or write is also forbidden.

1826

*Ira Frederick Aldridge, an African-American actor from New York, makes his London debut as Othello at the Royal Theatre in London. Aldridge becomes one of the greatest European actors of the nineteenth century.

1827

Freedom's Journal, the first African-American newspaper, begins publication in New York City.

1829

*Twelve hundred African Americans flee to Canada after a race riot in Cincinnati in which African-American citizens are attacked and their homes looted and burned.

*David Walker, a free African American, publishes an antislavery pamphlet *An Appeal to the Colored People of the World*. Walker's call for a slave revolt disturbs slaveholders.

1831

*Nat Turner leads the most successful slave revolt in history in Southampton County, Virginia. The South is alarmed by Turner's success and quickly moves to stop any other uprisings. Turner is captured and hanged in Jerusalem, Virginia.

1833

*The American Anti-Slavery Society is formed by both African-American and white abolitionists.

*Prudence Crandall is arrested in Canterbury, Connecticut, for operating a school for African-American girls.

*Oberlin College opens with an integrated student body. Oberlin becomes a meeting place for abolitionist causes.

1834

*Seven hundred thousand slaves are freed when slavery is abolished in the British Empire.

1839

*Joseph Cinque leads a slave rebellion aboard the ship the *Amistad*.

1841

*African captives revolt on board the *Creole*, which is sailing from Hampton, Virginia, to New Orleans. Revolt leaders sail the ship to the Bahamas. The Africans are given their freedom.

1844

*Explorer Jim Beckwourth discovers a route, now called Beckwourth Pass, through the Sierra Nevada Mountains to California and the Pacific Ocean.

1845

*Macon B. Allen becomes the first African-American lawyer admitted to the bar after passing his examination at Worcester, Massachusetts.

1846

*Norbert Rillieux patents the multiple-effect vacuum evaporation process, which changes the way sugar is processed.

1847
*Dred Scott, a slave, files suit for his freedom in the Circuit Court of St. Louis.

1848
*William and Ellen Craft escape from slavery in Maryland. Ellen, who is fair-skinned, dresses as a young white man. William acts as her servant.

1849
*Harriet Tubman escapes from slavery in Maryland.

1852
*Harriet Beecher Stowe's book *Uncle Tom's Cabin* is published in Boston.

1853
Clotel, written by William Wells Brown, becomes the first novel published by an African American.

1857
*Dred Scott loses his case to obtain his freedom before the Supreme Court by a six to three vote. The Court's decision opens federal territory to slavery, denies African Americans citizenship rights, and states that slaves do not become free when taken into a free territory.

1858
*U.S. attorney rules that slaves cannot patent their inventions because they are not citizens.

1859

*Abolitionist John Brown attacks Harpers Ferry, Virginia, with thirteen white men and five African Americans. Brown is later hanged at Charles Town, Virginia.

1861

*Southern Confederates attack Fort Sumter, South Carolina. This assault marks the beginning of the Civil War.

1862

*Robert Smalls sails the *Planter,* a Confederate boat, to freedom and presents it to the U.S. Navy.

*Congress approves African-American enlistment in the military service.

1863

*President Lincoln signs the Emancipation Proclamation, which frees slaves in all rebel states (except for a few parishes and counties in Louisiana, West Virginia, and eastern Virginia) and slaves in the Border States.

1865

*Confederate army surrenders, ending the Civil War.

*President Lincoln dies after being shot by John Wilkes Booth at Ford's Theater in Washington.

*Thirteenth Amendment, abolishing slavery in America, is passed.

1866

*The Civil Rights Bill and the Fourteenth Amendment, which give African Americans full rights as American citizens, are passed.

*African-American demonstrators in Charleston, Richmond, New Orleans, and other cities stage ride-ins on streetcars to protest segregation.

1870
*Hiram R. Revels of Mississippi is sworn in as the first African-American U.S. senator and the first African-American representative in Congress.

*Fifteenth Amendment, which guarantees the right to vote, is ratified.

1871
*P. B. S. Pinchback is elected acting lieutenant governor and president pro tem of the Louisiana senate.

1872
*Howard University student Charlotte E. Ray becomes the first African-American woman to graduate from a university law school in the United States.

1873
*P. B. S. Pinchback is elected to the U.S. Senate.

1877
*Henry O. Flipper becomes the first African-American graduate of West Point.

1879
*In the "Exodus of 1879" thousands of African Americans leave the South and settle in Kansas and other northern areas. Migrants are led by Benjamin "Pap" Singleton and Henry Adams.

1888
*The first African-American bank, Capital Savings Bank, opens in Washington, D.C.

1893
*Dr. Daniel Hale Williams performs the first successful open-heart operation, at Chicago's Provident Hospital.

1895
*Ida B. Wells-Barnett publishes *A Red Record,* the first statistical account of the lynchings of African Americans.

1896
*The *Plessy* v. *Ferguson* decision by the U.S. Supreme Court sanctions the "separate but equal" theory, beginning the Jim Crow years in America.

1898
*The Tenth Cavalry and other African-American military units fight during the Spanish-American War.

1903
*Maggie L. Walker becomes the first African-American woman bank president—director of the St. Luke Bank and Trust Company in Richmond, Virginia.

1904
*Educator Mary McLeod Bethune opens the Daytona Normal and Industrial School in Daytona Beach, Florida. The school merges with the Cookman Institute in 1923 and becomes Bethune-Cookman College.

1905

*W. E. B. Du Bois and William Monroe Trotter form the Niagara Movement. This organization later becomes the National Association for the Advancement of Colored People (NAACP).

1906

*African-American soldiers stationed in Brownsville, Texas, raid the town after a racial incident. President Theodore Roosevelt orders three companies of the Twenty-fifth Regiment dishonorably discharged for their alleged involvement in the raid.

1908

*Jack Johnson wins the heavyweight championship fight against Tommy Burns.

1909

*The NAACP is organized with forty-seven white members and six African Americans. The first NAACP conference is held at the United Charities Building in New York.

*African-American explorer Matthew Henson and Commander Robert E. Peary reach the North Pole.

1912

*"Memphis Blues" written by W. C. Handy, goes on sale in Memphis, Tennessee, and becomes the first published blues composition.

1915

*The Great Migration begins. During the next few decades more than 2 million southern African Americans will move to the North.

1917
*Ten thousand African Americans march silently down Fifth Avenue in New York City to protest lynchings and racial injustice in America.

1918
*African-American privates Henry Johnson and Needham Roberts of the 369th Infantry Regiment are the first American soldiers decorated for bravery during World War I in France.

1919
*Businesswoman Madame C. J. Walker dies after making a fortune selling beauty products especially created for African-American women.

*The summer of 1919 is called the "Red Summer" because of riots and bloodshed around the country as African Americans struggle for their civil rights. Seventy-six African Americans are reported lynched in 1919.

1925
*The Brotherhood of Sleeping Car Porters, a labor union formed to better the working conditions of African Americans employed by the railroad, is organized. A. Philip Randolph is elected president.

1926
*African-American historian Carter G. Woodson organizes the first Negro History Week. This celebration later becomes African-American History Month.

1936
*President Franklin Roosevelt appoints Mary McLeod Bethune as administrator of the new Office of Minority Affairs. Bethune

is the first African-American woman ever to hold a government job of this kind. Bethune becomes a good friend of Roosevelt's wife, Eleanor, and an important voice in the civil rights movement during the 1930s and 1940s.

*Jesse Owens wins four gold medals at the Olympic Games in Berlin, Germany.

1937
*William H. Hastie becomes the first African-American U.S. federal judge, presiding over the federal district court in the Virgin Islands.

*Joe Louis becomes heavyweight champion after defeating James J. Braddock.

1938
*Crystal Bird Fauset of Philadelphia is elected to the Pennsylvania legislature, the first African-American woman to become a legislator.

1939
*Opera singer Marian Anderson gives a concert at the Lincoln Memorial after the Daughters of the American Revolution refuse to let her sing in Constitution Hall because she is African American. More than seventy-five thousand African Americans and whites attend the Easter Sunday concert.

1940
*Frederick O'Neal and Abram Hill organize the American Negro Theatre.

*Benjamin Oliver Davis, Sr., becomes the first African-American general in the regular army.

1941

*The first Army Air Corps squadron for African-American cadets is formed. The first U.S. Army flying school for African-American cadets is dedicated at Tuskegee, Alabama.

*Sailor Dorie Miller of the USS *Arizona* mans a machine gun during the attack on Pearl Harbor and downs four Japanese planes. Miller was later awarded the Navy Cross.

1942

*John H. Johnson publishes the first issue of *Negro Digest*. Johnson later publishes *Ebony* and *Jet* magazines.

1948

*Ralph J. Bunche becomes United Nations mediator for peace in Palestine.

*Alice Coachman wins the running high jump and becomes the first African-American woman to win a gold medal in the Olympics.

1949

*The first African-American–owned radio station, WERD, opens in Atlanta.

1950

*Poet Gwendolyn Brooks becomes the first African American to win the Pulitzer Prize for her book of poems *Annie Allen*.

*Ralph J. Bunche is the first African American to be awarded the Nobel Peace Prize for his work in negotiating a peaceful end to the Palestine conflict in the Middle East.

1954

*The U.S. Supreme Court rules in *Brown* v. *Board of Education* that segregation in public schools is unconstitutional.

*Benjamin O. Davis, Jr., becomes the first African-American general in the air force.

1955

*Marian Anderson becomes the first African-American singer in the history of the Metropolitan Opera when she appears in Verdi's *Masked Ball.*

*NAACP member and seamstress Rosa Parks is arrested in Montgomery, Alabama, when she refuses to give up her bus seat to a white man.

*A bus boycott led by Martin Luther King, Jr., is organized at the Holt Street Baptist Church.

1956

*Martin Luther King's home is bombed.

*The U.S. Supreme Court upholds the lower court's decision that racial segregation on Montgomery buses violates the Constitution. Montgomery's African-American citizens end the yearlong bus boycott. Buses are integrated on December 21, 1956.

1957

*The Prayer Pilgrimage, a civil rights demonstration, is held in Washington, D.C.

*Nine African-American students are escorted by National Guard troops to integrate Central High School in Little Rock, Arkansas.

1959

*A Raisin in the Sun, the first Broadway play by an African-American woman (Lorraine Hansberry), opens at the Barrymore Theatre. The award-winning play has the first African-

American Broadway director, Lloyd Richards, and features Sidney Poitier and Claudia McNeil in the starring roles.

*Songwriter Berry Gordy starts Motown Records in Detroit.

1960
*Four African-American students from North Carolina A&T College start the sit-in movement when they refuse to leave a "whites only" Woolworth lunch counter without being served. The movement spreads across the United States.

*The Student Nonviolent Coordinating Committee (SNCC) is organized at Shaw University in Raleigh, North Carolina.

*President Dwight D. Eisenhower signs the Civil Rights Act of 1960.

1961
*Thurgood Marshall is appointed by President John F. Kennedy to the U.S. Circuit Court of Appeals.

*Thirteen freedom riders begin a bus trip through the South. Their bus is bombed and burned and the riders are attacked outside Anniston and Birmingham, Alabama.

1962
*Riots occur on the University of Mississippi campus when African-American student James H. Meredith attempts to register. Meredith is finally able to register with the assistance of federal marshals.

1963
*Carl T. Rowan is named ambassador to Finland.

*NAACP field secretary Medgar W. Evers is shot and killed in front of his home in Jackson, Mississippi.

*The Sixteenth Street Baptist Church of Birmingham, Alabama, is bombed. Four African-American girls are killed.

1964

*Dr. Martin Luther King, Jr., is awarded the Nobel Peace Prize. At thirty-five, King is the youngest person ever to receive the award.

1965

*Malcolm X is assassinated in the Audubon Ballroom in New York City by members of the Black Muslims.

*Civil rights protesters marching from Selma to Montgomery, Alabama, are attacked with billy clubs and tear gas by state troopers and sheriff's deputies.

*After a national protest about the treatment of the marchers, the Selma-to-Montgomery march is peacefully continued by Martin Luther King, Jr. A rally is held in front of the Alabama capitol.

*Patricia R. Harris becomes the first African-American woman ambassador after her appointment to Luxembourg.

*Vivian Malone becomes the first African-American student to graduate from the University of Alabama.

*A six-day riot in Watts, a ghetto section of Los Angeles, California, causes $35 million in property damage and thirty-four deaths.

1966

*Bill Russell becomes coach of the Boston Celtics. Russell is the first African-American professional basketball coach.

*Milton Olive, Jr., is awarded the Congressional Medal of Honor for bravery in Vietnam.

*U.S. district judge Constance Baker Motley becomes the first African-American woman on the federal bench.

*Huey Newton and Bobby Seale form the Black Panther party in Oakland, California.

*Massachusetts Republican Edward W. Brooke becomes the first African American elected to the U.S. Senate since Reconstruction.

1967

*Thurgood Marshall becomes the first African-American Supreme Court justice.

*Major Robert H. Lawrence, Jr., the first African-American astronaut candidate, is killed during a training flight.

1968

*Martin Luther King, Jr., is shot and killed in Memphis, Tennessee. His funeral is attended by three hundred thousand people. Riots start in more than one hundred cities.

*Congress passes the Civil Rights Bill banning racial discrimination in housing and providing protection for civil rights workers.

1971

*The Reverend Jesse Jackson starts People United to Save Humanity (PUSH) in Chicago.

1973

*Thomas Bradley is elected mayor of Los Angeles, California; Maynard Jackson is elected mayor of Atlanta, Georgia; and Coleman Young is elected mayor of Detroit, Michigan.

1974

*Henry "Hank" Aaron hits his 715th home run in Atlanta, breaking Babe Ruth's major league baseball record.

1975

*Singer/entertainer Josephine Baker dies at the age of sixty-eight in Paris.

*Golfer Lee Elder becomes the first African American to play in the Masters' Tournament.

*Arthur Ashe defeats Jimmy Connors at Wimbledon and wins the men's singles championship.

*Daniel "Chappie" James, Jr., is promoted to the rank of four-star general and is named commander in chief of the North American Air Defense Command.

1977

*Roots, a novel by Alex Haley, is shown as an eight-night mini-series presentation to 130 million television viewers.

1979

*Professor Arthur Lewis of Princeton becomes the first African American to win a Nobel Prize in economics.

1981

*Andrew Young becomes mayor of Atlanta, Georgia.

1983

*Miss New York State, Vanessa Williams, becomes the first African-American Miss America.

1984

*The release of navy lieutenant Robert O. Goodman, who was shot down and taken prisoner by Syria while on a mission over Lebanon, is negotiated by the Reverend Jesse Jackson.

1985

*Lieutenant Commander Donnie Cochran becomes the first African-American pilot in the U.S. Navy to fly with the Blue Angels, an elite precision aerobatics flight team.

1986

*Dr. Martin Luther King, Jr.'s birthday is celebrated as a federal holiday for the first time.

*Mrs. Coretta Scott King visits Archbishop Desmond Tutu and Winnie Mandela in South Africa.

1987

*Johnetta Cole is named president of Spelman College in Atlanta, Georgia.

1988

*Lee Roy Young becomes the first African-American Texas Ranger in the Texas Department of Public Safety's 165-year history.

1989

*Attorney Ronald H. Brown is elected the first African-American chairman of the Democratic National Committee.

1990

*L. Douglas Wilder of Virginia becomes the first African-American governor in the United States since Reconstruction.

*The Reverend Dr. Ralph David Abernathy, a close associate of

Dr. Martin Luther King, Jr., during the civil rights movement and former head of the Southern Christian Leadership Conference, dies on April 17.

1991

*Sharon Pratt Dixon is elected mayor of Washington, D.C. She becomes the first African-American woman mayor of a major city.

*Jazz trumpeter Miles Davis dies. Davis's fresh, innovative approach to traditional jazz began what is now known as "the birth of cool."

*The Reverend Jesse Jackson wins elective office for the first time, becoming the "shadow senator" from the District of Columbia. This gives Jackson a voice in Congress but no voting power.

*Judge Clarence Thomas is appointed to replace retired Supreme Court justice Thurgood Marshall.

*After announcing that he has tested positive for the HIV virus that causes the acquired immune deficiency syndrome (AIDS), basketball player Earvin "Magic" Johnson retires from the National Basketball Association's Los Angeles Lakers on November 7. Johnson becomes a national spokesman for AIDS awareness and prevention.

1992

*Alex Haley dies on February 10 at the age of seventy. Haley won a Pulitzer Prize for his book *Roots: The Saga of an American Family.*

*West Indian poet Derek Walcott wins the Nobel Prize for Literature for his poetry's "melodious and sensitive style."

1993

*Author Maya Angelou becomes the first black woman and the second poet since 1961 to be selected to read a poem at a presidential inaugural. Ms. Angelou recites her poem *On the Pulse of Morning* at the inauguration of President William Jefferson Clinton.

*Jazz trumpeter John Birks ("Dizzy") Gillespie dies of pancreatic cancer on January 6.

*Millionaire businessman Reginald F. Lewis dies on January 20 of brain cancer. Lewis, who purchased Beatrice International in 1987 for $985 million, was one of the most successful businessmen in modern times.

*Thomas A. Dorsey, known as the "father of gospel music" because of the more than one thousand religious songs he wrote and best known for the song *Take My Hand, Precious Lord*, dies of Alzheimer's disease on January 23. Dorsey, who also composed more than two thousand blues songs, combined blues and ragtime rhythms in his gospel compositions.

*Arthur Ashe, the only black man to win the Wimbledon Tennis Championship and the United States Open, and a civil rights activist, dies of AIDS on February 6. Ashe said that he was infected by a blood transfusion during heart-bypass surgery undergone in 1983.

SELECTED
BIBLIOGRAPHY

Adams, Russell. *Great Negroes: Past and Present*. Chicago: Afro-Am Publishing Company, 1984.

Ashe, Arthur R., Jr. *A Hard Road to Glory: A History of the African-American Athlete*. 3 vols. New York: Warner Books, 1988.

Bennett, Lerone, Jr. *Before the Mayflower—A History of Black America*. Chicago: Johnson Publishing Company, 1982.

Blockson, Charles L. *The Underground Railroad: First-Person Narratives of Escapes to Freedom in the North*. New York: Prentice Hall, 1987.

Bradford, Sarah. *Harriet Tubman: The Moses of Her People*. Secaucus, N.J.: Corinth Books, 1961.

Branch, Taylor. *Parting the Waters: America in the King Years 1954–1963*. New York: Simon and Schuster, 1968.

Conneau, Theophilus. *A Slaver's Logbook or 20 Years Residence in Africa*. Englewood Cliffs, N.J.: Prentice Hall, 1976.

Davidson, Basil. *Great Ages of Man: African Kingdoms*. New York: Time-Life Books, 1966.

Douglass, Frederick. Edited by Henry Louis Gates, Jr. *Narrative of the Life of Frederick Douglass, an American Slave*. 1845. In *The Classic Slave Narrative*. New York: Penguin Books, 1987.

Du Bois, W. E. B. *The Suppression of the African Slave Trade to the United States of America 1638–1870*. New York: Schocken Books, 1969.

Ebony magazine. *Ebony Pictorial History of Black America*. 3 vols. Chicago: Johnson Publishing Company, 1974.

Emillo, Luis. *History of the Fifty-fourth Regiment*. Boston: Boston Books Company, 1894.

Everett, Susanne. *History of Slavery*. London: Bison Books, 1978.

Franklin, John Hope. *From Slavery to Freedom*. 6th ed. New York: McGraw-Hill, 1988.

Haber, Louis. *Black Pioneers of Science and Invention*. New York: Harcourt, Brace and World, 1970.

Harris, Middleton, et al. *The Black Book*. New York: Random House, 1974.

Henri, Florette. *Black Migration: Movement North 1900–1920*. Garden City, N.Y.: Anchor Press, 1975.

Higgins, Chester, Jr., and Orde Coombs. *Some Time Ago—A Historic Portrait of Black Americans, 1850–1950*. New York: Anchor Press, 1980.

Hughes, Langston, Milton Meltzer, and C. Eric Lincoln. *A Pictorial History of Black Americans*. New York: Crown Publishers, 1983.

Hurston, Zora Neale. *Dust Tracks on a Road: An Autobiography*. Champaign: University of Illinois Press, 1984.

Jones, Howard. *Mutiny on the* Amistad: *The Saga of a Slave Revolt and Its Impact on American Abolition, Law and Diplomacy*. New York: Oxford University Press, 1987.

Kaplan, Sidney. *The Black Presence in the Era of the American Revolution, 1770–1800*. Washington, D.C.: Smithsonian Institution Press, 1973.

Katz, William Loren. *The Black West*. Seattle: Open Hand Publishing, 1987.

———. *Minorities in American History*. 4 vols. New York: Watts, 1974.

Lewis, David L. *When Harlem Was in Vogue*. New York: Vintage Books, 1982.

Logan, Rayford W., and Michael R. Winston, eds. *Dictionary of American Negro Biography*. New York: W. W. Norton and Company, 1982.

Love, Nat. *The Life and Adventures of Nat Love*. New York: Arno Press, 1968.

Low, W. Augustus, and Virgil A. Clift. *Encyclopedia of Black America*. New York: Da Capo Press, 1981.

Ploski, Harry A., and James Williams. *The Negro Almanac: A Reference Work on the African American.* Detroit: Gale Research, 1989.

Richardson, Ben, and William A. Fahey. *Great Black Americans.* New York: Thomas Y. Crowell Company, 1976.

Rogers, J. A. *Africa's Gift to America.* New York: H. M. Rogers, 1961.

Rose, Willie Lee. *A Documentary History of Slavery in North America.* New York: Oxford University Press, 1976.

Schulke, F., and P. O. McPhee. *King Remembered: A Biography, a Photo Essay, a Tribute.* New York: W. W. Norton and Company, 1986.

Stampp, Kenneth M. *The Peculiar Institution: Slavery in the Ante-Bellum South.* New York: Vintage Books, 1956.

Sterling, Dorothy. *Black Foremothers: Three Lives.* 2nd ed. New York: Feminist Press, 1988.

Wells-Barnett, Ida B. *Crusade for Justice.* Edited by Alfreda M. Duster. Chicago: University of Chicago Press, 1970.

Wheat, Ellen Harkins. *Jacob Lawrence, American Painter.* Seattle: University of Washington Press and the Seattle Art Museum, 1986.

Books for Young Readers

Cox, Clinton. *Undying Glory: The Story of the Massachusetts 54th Regiment.* New York: Scholastic, 1991.

Katz, William Loren. *Breaking the Chains: African-American Slave Resistance.* New York: Atheneum, 1990.

Lester, Julius. *To Be A Slave.* New York: Dial Press, 1968.

———. *This Strange New Feeling.* New York: Dial Press, 1982.

McKissack, Patricia, and Frederick McKissack. *The Civil Rights Movement in America: From 1865 to the Present.* Chicago: Children's Press, 1987.

———. *Martin Luther King, Jr.* Chicago: Children's Press, 1984.

Myers, Walter Dean. *Now Is Your Time! The African-American Struggle for Freedom.* New York: Harper Collins Publishers, 1991.

Smead, Howard. *The Afro-Americans.* New York: Chelsea House Publishers, 1989.

Spangley, Earl. *The Blacks in America.* Minneapolis: Lerner Publications, 1987.

Index